Daily 6-Trait Writing GRADE 3

DISCARD

Editorial Development: Barbara Allman
Roseann Erwin
Joy Evans
Leslie Sorg
Andrea Weiss
Copy Editing: Cathy Harber
Art Direction: Cheryl Puckett
Cover Design: Liliana Potigian
Illustrators: Lauren Scheuer
Len Borozinski
Design/Production: Carolina Caird

EMC 6023

Evan-Moor
EDUCATIONAL PUBLISHERS
Helping Children Learn since 1979

Congratulations on your purchase of some of the finest teaching materials in the world.

Correlated to State Standards

Contents

Daily 6-Trait Writing • EMC 6023 • © Evan-Moor Corp.

Daily 6-Trait Writing contains 25 weeks of mini-lessons divided into five units. Each unit provides five weeks of scaffolded instruction focused on one of the following traits: **Ideas, Organization, Word Choice, Sentence Fluency,** and **Voice.** (See pages 6–9 for more information about each of these, as well as the sixth trait, **Conventions.**) You may wish to teach each entire unit in consecutive order, or pick and choose the lessons within the unit.

Each week of *Daily 6-Trait Writing* focuses on a specific skill within the primary trait, as well as one Convention skill. The weeks follow a consistent five-day format, making *Daily 6-Trait Writing* easy to use.

Teacher Overview Pages

Trait Skill

A specific writing skill for each trait is targeted.

Reduced Pages

Reduced student pages provide sample answers.

Convention Skill

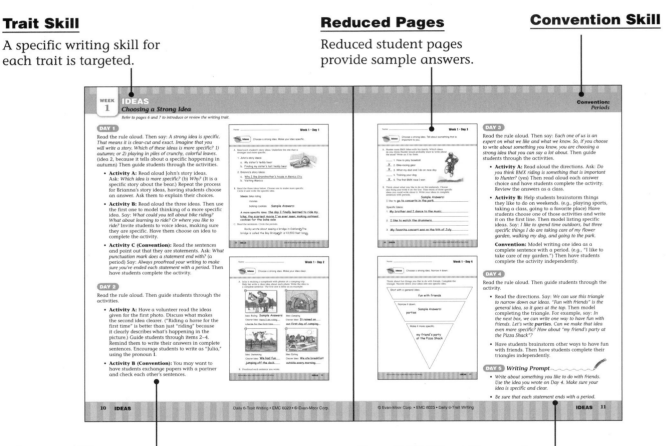

Lesson Plans

Use the lesson plans to teach the trait and Convention skills and guide students through the activities on Days 1–4. The plans are structured to enable you to differentiate and tailor lessons for your own class, but still provide the explanation and support you need. You may choose to have students complete the activities as a class, in small groups, or independently.

Day 5 Writing Prompt

Give your students the writing prompt to apply the trait and Convention skills in their own writing. Provide students with paper, or use the page provided for Day 5 in the student practice book. You may also wish to expand the writing prompt into a more fully developed assignment that takes students through the writing process.

Student Activity Pages

Trait and Rule (Skill Summary)

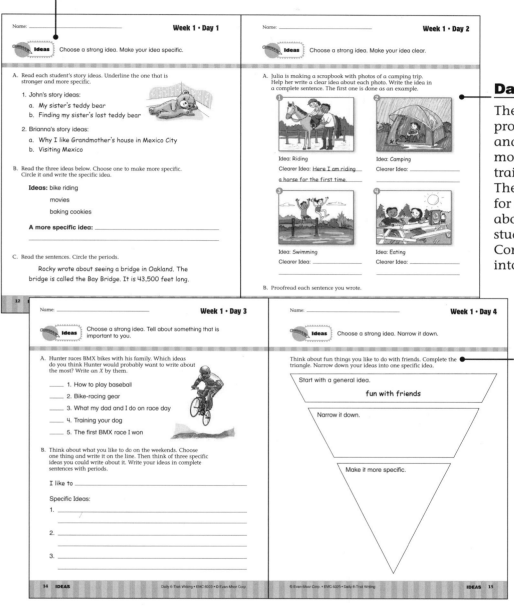

Name: _____ Week 1 • Day 1

Ideas Choose a strong idea. Make your idea specific.

A. Read each student's story ideas. Underline the one that is stronger and more specific.

1. John's story ideas:
   a. My sister's teddy bear
   b. Finding my sister's lost teddy bear

2. Brianna's story ideas:
   a. Why I like Grandmother's house in Mexico City
   b. Visiting Mexico

B. Read the three ideas below. Choose one to make more specific. Circle it and write the specific idea.

Ideas: bike riding

movies

baking cookies

A more specific idea: _____

C. Read the sentences. Circle the periods.

Rocky wrote about seeing a bridge in Oakland. The bridge is called the Bay Bridge. It is 43,500 feet long.

Name: _____ Week 1 • Day 2

Ideas Choose a strong idea. Make your idea clear.

A. Julia is making a scrapbook with photos of a camping trip. Help her write a clear idea about each photo. Write the idea in a complete sentence. The first one is done as an example.

① Idea: Riding
Clearer Idea: Here I am riding a horse for the first time.

② Idea: Camping
Clearer Idea: _____

③ Idea: Swimming
Clearer Idea: _____

④ Idea: Eating
Clearer Idea: _____

B. Proofread each sentence you wrote.

Days 1–3 Activities

The activities on Days 1–3 provide models for students to analyze, revise, or add to. These models expose students to the traits in many forms of writing. They also provide opportunities for students to think critically about writing, enhancing students' own proficiency. The Convention skill is integrated into the activities.

Name: _____ Week 1 • Day 3

Ideas Choose a strong idea. Tell about something that is important to you.

A. Hunter races BMX bikes with his family. Which ideas do you think Hunter would probably want to write about the most? Write an X by them.

_____ 1. How to play baseball

_____ 2. Bike-racing gear

_____ 3. What my dad and I do on race day

_____ 4. Training your dog

_____ 5. The first BMX race I won

B. Think about what you like to do on the weekends. Choose one thing and write it on the line. Then think of three specific ideas you could write about it. Write your ideas in complete sentences with periods.

I like to _____

Specific Ideas:

1. _____

2. _____

3. _____

Name: _____ Week 1 • Day 4

Ideas Choose a strong idea. Narrow it down.

Think about fun things you like to do with friends. Complete the triangle. Narrow down your ideas into one specific idea.

Start with a general idea.
fun with friends

Narrow it down.

Make it more specific.

Day 4 Activity

The Day 4 activity provides a prewriting form for the Day 5 writing prompt.

Ways to Use

There are many ways to integrate *Daily 6-Trait Writing* into your classroom:

- Teach the lessons trait by trait.
- Target and practice specific skills students need help with.
- Use the lessons to enhance writing workshops.
- Incorporate the lessons into your other writing programs.

Use these ideas to introduce or review the trait at the beginning of each unit.

Ideas

Explain to students that good writing starts with good ideas.

Say: *A good idea is clear, interesting, and original. It makes the reader say, "Wow!" or "I never would have thought of that!" Without good ideas, your writing would not have much of a point. Your reader would be bored!*

Organization

Explain to students that good writing is organized in a way that helps the reader understand the information and follow what the writer is saying.

Say: *The organization of your writing is what holds everything together. It puts your ideas in an order that makes sense, and it gives your writing a strong beginning, middle, and end. When your writing is not organized, your reader can grow confused and lose interest.*

Word Choice

Explain to students that good writers choose their words carefully in order to get their ideas across.

Say: *When you write, choose just the right words and use them correctly. Make them fun and interesting so they help your readers "see" what you are talking about. Try not to use the same words over and over again. If you don't choose your words carefully, your reader may not understand what you're trying to say.*

Sentence Fluency

Explain to students that good writers make their writing flow by using different kinds of sentences.

Say: *You want your writing to be easy to read and follow. It should flow so smoothly and sound so interesting that people want to read it aloud! When your sentences don't flow, your writing sounds choppy and flat. Your reader would not want to read it aloud.*

Voice

Explain to students that when they write, their personality, or who they are, should shine through.

Say: *You want your writing to sound like you, and no one else! When you write, you show who you are through words. No matter what type of writing you do, always make sure it sounds like you. Otherwise, your reader may not care about what you have to say. In fact, your reader may not even know who wrote it!*

Conventions

Explain to students that good writers follow all the rules, or conventions, of writing, so their readers can easily read and understand the writing.

Say: *Using correct grammar, spelling, and punctuation when you write is important. When you don't follow the rules, your reader can become lost or confused. He or she may not know where one idea starts and another begins.*

Using the Rubric

Use the rubric on pages 8 and 9 to evaluate and assess your students' skill acquisition.

- Each week, evaluate students' responses to the Day 5 writing prompt using the criteria that correspond to the skills taught that week.

- For Week 5, use all the trait criteria to assess students' understanding of that trait as a whole.

- Use the entire set of criteria to occasionally assess students' writing across the traits.

- In student- and parent-teacher conferences, use the rubric to accurately and clearly explain what a student does well in writing, as well as what he or she needs to improve.

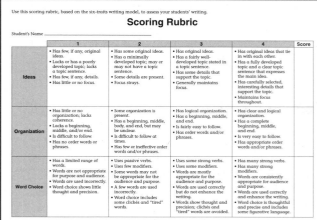

Use this scoring rubric, based on the six-traits writing model, to assess your students' writing.

Scoring Rubric

Student's Name _____

	1	2	3	4	Score
Ideas	• Has few, if any, original ideas. • Lacks or has a poorly developed topic; lacks a topic sentence. • Has few, if any, details. • Has little or no focus.	• Has some original ideas. • Has a minimally developed topic; may or may not have a topic sentence. • Some details are present. • Focus strays.	• Has original ideas. • Has a fairly well-developed topic stated in a topic sentence. • Has some details that support the topic. • Generally maintains focus.	• Has original ideas that tie in with each other. • Has a fully developed topic and a clear topic sentence that expresses the main idea. • Has carefully selected, interesting details that support the topic. • Maintains focus throughout.	
Organization	• Has little or no organization; lacks coherence. • Lacks a beginning, middle, and/or end. • Is difficult to follow. • Has no order words or phrases.	• Some organization is present. • Has a beginning, middle, body, and end, but may be unclear. • Is difficult to follow at times. • Has few or ineffective order words and/or phrases.	• Has logical organization. • Has a beginning, middle, and end. • Is fairly easy to follow. • Has order words and/or phrases.	• Has clear and logical organization. • Has a complete beginning, middle, and end. • Is very easy to follow. • Has appropriate order words and/or phrases.	
Word Choice	• Has a limited range of words. • Words are not appropriate for purpose and audience. • Words are used incorrectly. • Word choice shows little thought and precision.	• Uses passive verbs. • Uses few modifiers. • Some words may not be appropriate for the audience and purpose. • A few words are used incorrectly. • Word choice includes some clichés and "tired" words.	• Uses some strong verbs. • Uses some modifiers. • Words are mostly appropriate for the audience and purpose. • Words are used correctly but do not enhance the writing. • Words show thought and precision; clichés and "tired" words are avoided.	• Has many strong verbs. • Has many strong modifiers. • Words are consistently appropriate for audience and purpose. • Words are used correctly and enhance the writing. • Word choice is thoughtful and precise and includes some figurative language.	

Sentence Fluency	• Does not write complete sentences. • Writes only run-on or rambling sentences. • Has no variation in sentence structures and lengths. • Has no variation in sentence beginnings. • Has no cadence or flow in sentences.	• Has some incomplete sentences. • Has some run-on or rambling sentences. • Has little variation in sentence structures and lengths. • Has little variation in sentence beginnings. • Sentences flow somewhat.	• Has 1 or 2 incomplete sentences. • Has 1 or 2 run-on or rambling sentences. • Has some variation in sentence structures and lengths. • Has some variation in sentence beginnings. • Sentences flow fairly naturally.	• Has complete sentences. • Has no run-on or rambling sentences. • Varied sentence structures and lengths contribute to the rhythm of the writing. • Varied sentence beginnings contribute to the flow of the writing. • Sentences flow naturally.
Voice	• Writing is neither expressive nor engaging. • Voice is not appropriate for the purpose, audience, topic, and/or genre. • Little evidence of an individual voice.	• Writing has some expression. • Voice is generally appropriate for the purpose, audience, topic, and/or genre. • Voice comes and goes.	• Writing is expressive and somewhat engaging. • Voice is appropriate for the purpose, audience, topic, and/or genre. • The voice is unique.	• Writing is very expressive and engaging. • Voice is consistently appropriate for the purpose, audience, topic, and/or genre. • The voice is unique, honest, and passionate.
Conventions	• Has multiple errors in grammar, punctuation, and mechanics. • Poor handwriting and/or presentation makes the writing hard to read. • Illustrations, if present, do not accurately portray the main idea.	• Has some errors in grammar, punctuation, and mechanics. • Handwriting and/or presentation is fairly clear. • Illustrations, if present, portray the main idea but do not enhance it.	• Has few errors in grammar, punctuation, and mechanics. • Handwriting and/or presentation is clear. • Illustrations, if present, accurately portray the main idea and enhance it somewhat.	• Has minimal errors in grammar, punctuation, and mechanics. • Handwriting and/or presentation of the piece is attractive and easy to read. • Illustrations, if present, enhance the main idea significantly.

TOTAL

IDEAS
Choosing a Strong Idea

Refer to pages 6 and 7 to introduce or review the writing trait.

DAY 1

Read the rule aloud. Then say: *A strong idea is specific. That means it is clear-cut and exact. Imagine that you will write a story. Which of these ideas is more specific? 1) autumn; or 2) playing in piles of crunchy, colorful leaves.* (idea 2, because it tells about a specific happening in autumn) Then guide students through the activities.

- **Activity A:** Read aloud John's story ideas. Ask: *Which idea is more specific? (b) Why?* (It is a specific story about the bear.) Repeat the process for Brianna's story ideas, having students choose an answer. Ask them to explain their choices.

- **Activity B:** Read aloud the three ideas. Then use the first one to model thinking of a more specific idea. Say: *What could you tell about bike riding? What about learning to ride? Or where you like to ride?* Invite students to voice ideas, making sure they are specific. Have them choose an idea to complete the activity.

- **Activity C (Convention):** Read the sentences and point out that they are statements. Ask: *What punctuation mark does a statement end with?* (a period) Say: *Always proofread your writing to make sure you've ended each statement with a period.* Then have students complete the activity.

DAY 2

Read the rule aloud. Then guide students through the activities.

- **Activity A:** Have a volunteer read the ideas given for the first photo. Discuss what makes the second idea clearer. ("Riding a horse for the first time" is better than just "riding" because it clearly describes what's happening in the picture.) Guide students through items 2–4. Remind them to write their answers in complete sentences. Encourage students to write as "Julia," using the pronoun I.

- **Activity B (Convention):** You may want to have students exchange papers with a partner and check each other's sentences.

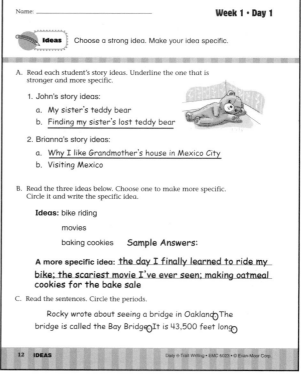

Name: _____ Week 1 • Day 1

Ideas Choose a strong idea. Make your idea specific.

A. Read each student's story ideas. Underline the one that is stronger and more specific.

1. John's story ideas:
   a. My sister's teddy bear
   b. Finding my sister's lost teddy bear

2. Brianna's story ideas:
   a. Why I like Grandmother's house in Mexico City
   b. Visiting Mexico

B. Read the three ideas below. Choose one to make more specific. Circle it and write the specific idea.

Ideas: bike riding

movies

baking cookies   **Sample Answers:**

A more specific idea: the day I finally learned to ride my bike; the scariest movie I've ever seen; making oatmeal cookies for the bake sale

C. Read the sentences. Circle the periods.

Rocky wrote about seeing a bridge in Oakland. The bridge is called the Bay Bridge. It is 43,500 feet long.

12 IDEAS   Daily 6-Trait Writing • EMC 6023 • © Evan-Moor Corp.

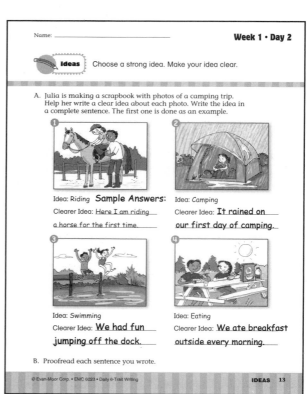

Name: _____ Week 1 • Day 2

Ideas Choose a strong idea. Make your idea clear.

A. Julia is making a scrapbook with photos of a camping trip. Help her write a clear idea about each photo. Write the idea in a complete sentence. The first one is done as an example.

Idea: Riding **Sample Answers:** Idea: Camping
Clearer Idea: Here I am riding a horse for the first time.   Clearer Idea: It rained on our first day of camping.

Idea: Swimming   Idea: Eating
Clearer Idea: We had fun jumping off the dock.   Clearer Idea: We ate breakfast outside every morning.

B. Proofread each sentence you wrote.

© Evan-Moor Corp. • EMC 6023 • Daily 6-Trait Writing   IDEAS 13

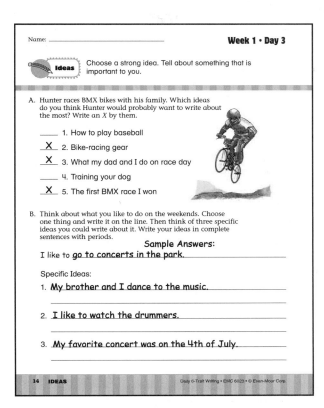

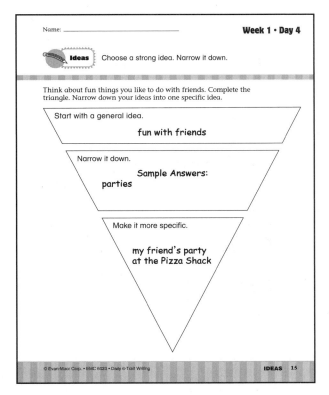

DAY 3

Read the rule aloud. Then say: *Each one of us is an expert on what we like and what we know. So, if you choose to write about something you know, you are choosing a strong idea that you can say a lot about.* Then guide students through the activities.

- **Activity A:** Read aloud the directions. Ask: *Do you think BMX riding is something that is important to Hunter?* (yes) Then read aloud each answer choice and have students complete the activity. Review the answers as a class.

- **Activity B:** Help students brainstorm things they like to do on weekends. (e.g., playing sports, taking a class, going to a favorite place) Have students choose one of those activities and write it on the first line. Then model listing specific ideas. Say: *I like to spend time outdoors, but three specific things I do are taking care of my flower garden, walking my dog, and going to the park.*

  Convention: Model writing one idea as a complete sentence with a period. (e.g., "I like to take care of my garden.") Then have students complete the activity independently.

DAY 4

Read the rule aloud. Then guide students through the activity.

- Read the directions. Say: *We can use this triangle to narrow down our ideas. "Fun with friends" is the general idea, so it goes at the top.* Then model completing the triangle. For example, say: *In the next box, we can write one way to have fun with friends. Let's write* **parties**. *Can we make that idea even more specific? How about "my friend's party at the Pizza Shack"?*

- Have students brainstorm other ways to have fun with friends. Then have students complete their triangles independently.

DAY 5 *Writing Prompt*

- *Write about something you like to do with friends. Use the idea you wrote on Day 4. Make sure your idea is specific and clear.*

- *Be sure that each statement ends with a period.*

 **Ideas**   Choose a strong idea. Make your idea specific.

A. Read each student's story ideas. Underline the one that is
    stronger and more specific.

1. John's story ideas:

    a. My sister's teddy bear

    b. Finding my sister's lost teddy bear

2. Brianna's story ideas:

    a. Why I like Grandmother's house in Mexico City

    b. Visiting Mexico

B. Read the three ideas below. Choose one to make more specific.
    Circle it and write the specific idea.

    Ideas: bike riding

    movies

    baking cookies

    A more specific idea: _____

    _____

C. Read the sentences. Circle the periods.

    Rocky wrote about seeing a bridge in Oakland. The
    bridge is called the Bay Bridge. It is 43,500 feet long.

 **Ideas** Choose a strong idea. Make your idea clear.

A. Julia is making a scrapbook with photos of a camping trip. Help her write a clear idea about each photo. Write the idea in a complete sentence. The first one is done as an example.

Idea: Riding

Clearer Idea: <u>Here I am riding</u>

<u>a horse for the first time.</u>

Idea: Camping

Clearer Idea: _____

_____

Idea: Swimming

Clearer Idea: _____

_____

Idea: Eating

Clearer Idea: _____

_____

B. Proofread each sentence you wrote.

 **Ideas**

Choose a strong idea. Tell about something that is important to you.

A. Hunter races BMX bikes with his family. Which ideas do you think Hunter would probably want to write about the most? Write an *X* by them.

_____ 1. How to play baseball

_____ 2. Bike-racing gear

_____ 3. What my dad and I do on race day

_____ 4. Training your dog

_____ 5. The first BMX race I won

B. Think about what you like to do on the weekends. Choose one thing and write it on the line. Then think of three specific ideas you could write about it. Write your ideas in complete sentences with periods.

I like to _____

Specific Ideas:

1. _____

_____

2. _____

_____

3. _____

_____

 **Ideas** : Choose a strong idea. Narrow it down.

Think about fun things you like to do with friends. Complete the triangle. Narrow down your ideas into one specific idea.

Start with a general idea.

fun with friends

Narrow it down.

Make it more specific.

DAY 1

Review the concept of **main idea** by saying: *A main idea tells what a piece of writing is mostly about. The main idea is expressed in what is called a topic sentence.* Read the rule aloud. Then guide students through the activities.

- **Activity A (Convention):** Read the report aloud. Ask: *What is the topic sentence of this paragraph?* (the first sentence) Have students circle it. Then ask: *What should every sentence begin with?* (a capital letter) Say: *Some of the sentences in this paragraph are missing a capital letter. Can you find them?* Model using proofreading marks to indicate which letters should be capitalized.

- **Activity B:** Read the paragraph aloud. Ask: *What is the main idea?* (e.g., Where the Wild Things Are is a story about a boy.) Then say: *Be sure to include the main idea in your topic sentence.* Have students complete the activity on their own or in pairs. Then ask a few students to read aloud their topic sentences.

- **Activity C (Convention):** Have students use proofreading marks to fix the sentences in Activity B that do not begin with a capital letter. To check students' answers, read the report in Activity B aloud. Have students raise their hands each time a sentence needs a capital letter.

DAY 2

Read the rule aloud. Then guide students through the activities.

- **Activity A (Convention):** Ask: *What form of writing is this?* (friendly letter) Say: *Letters, like other forms of writing, should have a topic sentence in each paragraph.*

  Read aloud the letter as a group, or allow time for students to read silently. Instruct students to circle the paragraph that is missing its topic sentence. (the second one) Then guide students in fixing letters that should be capitalized.

- **Activity B:** Have students complete the activity on their own or in pairs. Have a few students read aloud their topic sentences.

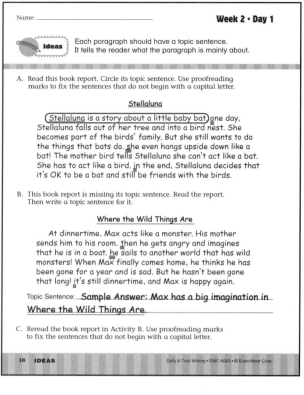

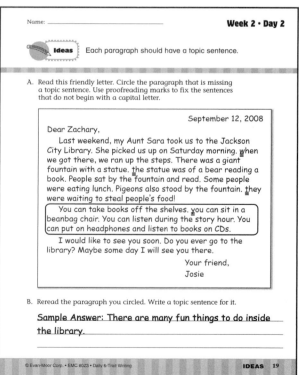

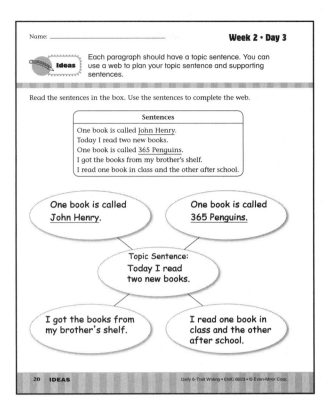

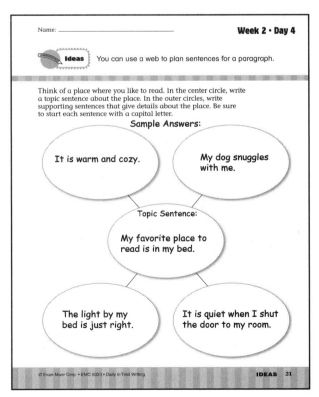

DAY 3

Read the rule aloud. Review main ideas and topic sentences. Explain that a **supporting sentence** is a sentence that gives details about the main idea. Then guide students through the activity.

- Have students read the sentences in the box. Ask: *Which is the topic sentence?* ("Today I read two new books.") Have students write the topic sentence in the middle of the web.

- Say: *The remaining sentences are supporting sentences. What do they tell us?* (details about the books) Say: *Write the supporting sentences in the circles around the topic sentence.*

- **Convention:** Have students check that they capitalized the first word of each sentence in their webs. Then model using the sentences to write a paragraph on the board. Have students suggest the order in which to write the sentences.

DAY 4

Read the rule aloud. Then guide students through the activity.

- Have students name some places they like to read. (e.g., library, bed, outside) Model turning one of the ideas into a topic sentence, such as: *My favorite place to read is in bed.* Then have students write their own topic sentences in the center circle, beginning with "My favorite place..."

- Say: *For the outer circles, think about what is in that place, how it makes you feel, and why you like it.* Model forming supporting sentences, such as: *I read under the covers. They make me feel warm and cozy.* Have students write their own supporting sentences. Check students' choice of details.

- **Convention:** Ask: *Have you started each sentence with a capital letter?* Have students make corrections as necessary.

DAY 5 *Writing Prompt*

- *Write a paragraph that describes your favorite place to go to read. Use the web you created on Day 4.*

- *Be sure to begin each sentence with a capital letter.*

 **Ideas** Each paragraph should have a topic sentence.
It tells the reader what the paragraph is mainly about.

A. Read this book report. Circle its topic sentence. Use proofreading marks to fix the sentences that do not begin with a capital letter.

Stellaluna

<u>Stellaluna</u> is a story about a little baby bat. one day, Stellaluna falls out of her tree and into a bird nest. She becomes part of the birds' family. But she still wants to do the things that bats do. she even hangs upside down like a bat! The mother bird tells Stellaluna she can't act like a bat. She has to act like a bird. in the end, Stellaluna decides that it's OK to be a bat and still be friends with the birds.

B. This book report is missing its topic sentence. Read the report. Then write a topic sentence for it.

Where the Wild Things Are

At dinnertime, Max acts like a monster. His mother sends him to his room. then he gets angry and imagines that he is in a boat. he sails to another world that has wild monsters! When Max finally comes home, he thinks he has been gone for a year and is sad. But he hasn't been gone that long! it's still dinnertime, and Max is happy again.

Topic Sentence: _____

_____

C. Reread the book report in Activity B. Use proofreading marks to fix the sentences that do not begin with a capital letter.

 Daily 6-Trait Writing • EMC 6023 • © Evan-Moor Corp.

 **Ideas**   Each paragraph should have a topic sentence.

A. Read this friendly letter. Circle the paragraph that is missing a topic sentence. Use proofreading marks to fix the sentences that do not begin with a capital letter.

September 12, 2008

Dear Zachary,

   Last weekend, my Aunt Sara took us to the Jackson City Library. She picked us up on Saturday morning. when we got there, we ran up the steps. There was a giant fountain with a statue. the statue was of a bear reading a book. People sat by the fountain and read. Some people were eating lunch. Pigeons also stood by the fountain. they were waiting to steal people's food!

   You can take books off the shelves. you can sit in a beanbag chair. You can listen during the story hour. You can put on headphones and listen to books on CDs.

   I would like to see you soon. Do you ever go to the library? Maybe some day I will see you there.

                              Your friend,

                              Josie

B. Reread the paragraph you circled. Write a topic sentence for it.

_____

_____

_____

 **Ideas** Each paragraph should have a topic sentence. You can use a web to plan your topic sentence and supporting sentences.

Read the sentences in the box. Use the sentences to complete the web.

Sentences

One book is called <u>John Henry</u>.
Today I read two new books.
One book is called <u>365 Penguins</u>.
I got the books from my brother's shelf.
I read one book in class and the other after school.

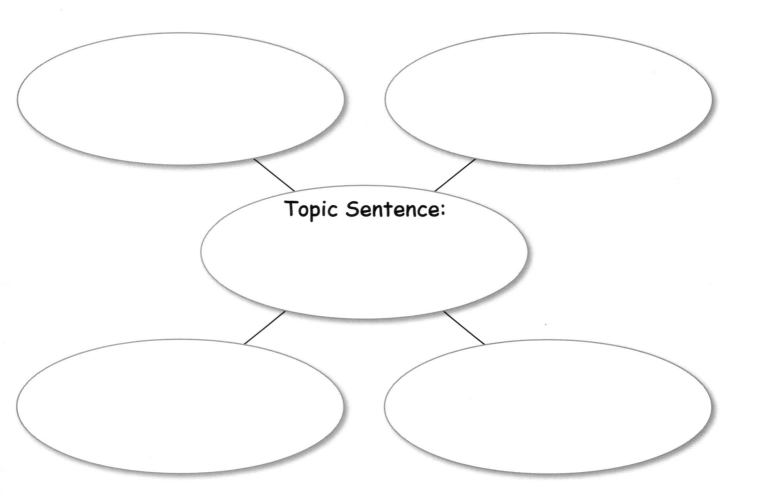

Topic Sentence:

 **Ideas** You can use a web to plan sentences for a paragraph.

Think of a place where you like to read. In the center circle, write a topic sentence about the place. In the outer circles, write supporting sentences that give details about the place. Be sure to start each sentence with a capital letter.

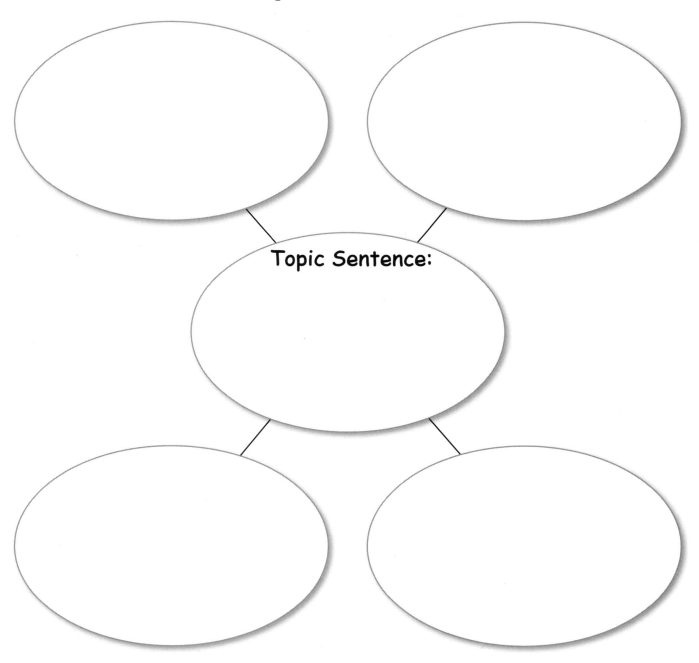

Topic Sentence:

DAY 1

Read the rule aloud. Then say: *Details are ideas that make our writing more interesting. Some details tell* **who** *and others tell* **what**. **Who** *and* **what** *are two of the "5 W" details.* Ask: *Do you know what the others are?* (**when, where, why**) Then guide students through the activities.

- **Activity A:** Read the articles together. Say: *A good* **who** *detail might give the name of someone.* Ask: *Which article has names of people?* ("News from Room 12") Then say: *A good* **what** *detail gives the name of a specific thing.* Ask: *Which is a more specific* **what** *detail: "we" or "all the third-grade classes"?* ("all the third-grade classes") Have students draw a star next to the article with interesting details.

- **Activity B:** Have students complete the activity independently. Then review the answers. For item 4, point out that the students' names are both **what** and **who**. They tell **what** was found in the dictionary. But they also tell **who** is in the class.

DAY 2

Read the rule aloud. Then say: *Yesterday, we learned about* **who** *and* **what**. *Today, we'll learn about the other three Ws:* **when, where,** *and* **why.** Then guide students through the activities.

- **Activity A:** Have students read the paragraph. Then ask: *What kind of detail is "one hundred years ago"?* (a **when** detail) Have students circle it. Continue guiding students through the paragraph, circling and underlining the details.

- **Activity B:** Help students brainstorm details by asking: *What do you do at different times of the day? When is your favorite time? Where do you go?* Help students form complete sentences.

- **Activity C (Convention):** Explain: *A contraction is a word formed from two words by leaving out some letters. Many contractions are made with the word* **not**. *An apostrophe takes the place of the missing* **o**. Help students brainstorm a list of contractions made with **not**, such as **doesn't, didn't, wasn't, weren't,** and **isn't**. Then have students find the contractions in the paragraph and write them.

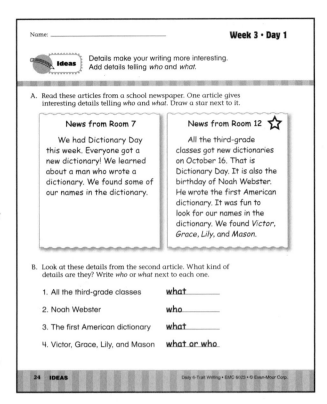

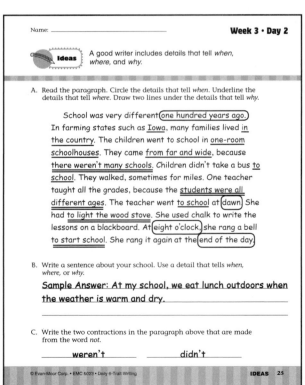

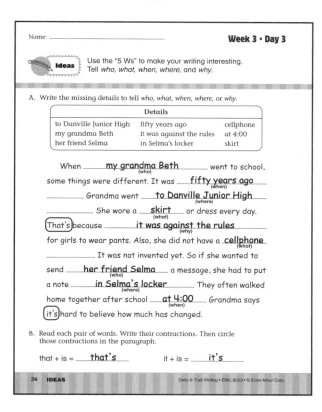

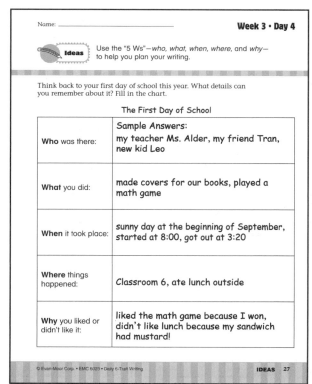

DAY 3

Read the rule aloud. Then guide students through the activities.

- **Activity A:** Have students read the words and phrases in the box. Then read aloud the first sentence. Ask: *Which **who** word or phrase makes sense with this sentence?* ("my grandma Beth") Have students complete the paragraph on their own. Then go over the answers as a class.

- **Activity B (Convention):** Review the definition of a contraction. Then say: *Many contractions are formed from the word **is**. The apostrophe takes the place of the **i**.* On the board, write **what + is = what's**. Say: ***What** and **is** form the contraction **what's**.* Have students brainstorm additional contractions made from **is**. (**that's, it's, she's**, etc.) Then have students complete the activity.

DAY 4

Read the rule aloud. Then guide students through the activity.

- Ask questions to help students brainstorm ideas. For example, ask: *Did you meet anyone new that day? Did you get any new school supplies? Where did you sit? Did we do anything special on that day?*

- You may want to have students work in pairs, using the "5 Ws" to ask each other questions. For example: *Whom did you talk to that day? What did you do at recess?*

- After students have completed their charts, invite volunteers to share what they wrote.

DAY 5 *Writing Prompt*

- *Use the details from your chart on Day 4 to write about the first day of school this year.*

- *Use a contraction made from **not** or **is**, such as **didn't** or **that's**. Be sure to use an apostrophe.*

Ideas

Details make your writing more interesting.
Add details telling *who* and *what*.

A. Read these articles from a school newspaper. One article gives
    interesting details telling *who* and *what*. Draw a star next to it.

News from Room 7

We had Dictionary Day
this week. Everyone got a
new dictionary! We learned
about a man who wrote a
dictionary. We found some of
our names in the dictionary.

News from Room 12

All the third-grade
classes got new dictionaries
on October 16. That is
Dictionary Day. It is also the
birthday of Noah Webster.
He wrote the first American
dictionary. It was fun to
look for our names in the
dictionary. We found *Victor*,
Grace, *Lily*, and *Mason*.

B. Look at these details from the second article. What kind of
    details are they? Write *who* or *what* next to each one.

1. All the third-grade classes   _____

2. Noah Webster   _____

3. The first American dictionary   _____

4. Victor, Grace, Lily, and Mason   _____

 **Ideas**   A good writer includes details that tell *when, where,* and *why.*

A. Read the paragraph. Circle the details that tell *when*. Underline the details that tell *where*. Draw two lines under the details that tell *why*.

School was very different one hundred years ago. In farming states such as Iowa, many families lived in the country. The children went to school in one-room schoolhouses. They came from far and wide, because there weren't many schools. Children didn't take a bus to school. They walked, sometimes for miles. One teacher taught all the grades, because the students were all different ages. The teacher went to school at dawn. She had to light the wood stove. She used chalk to write the lessons on a blackboard. At eight o'clock, she rang a bell to start school. She rang it again at the end of the day.

B. Write a sentence about your school. Use a detail that tells *when, where,* or *why.*

_____

_____

_____

C. Write the two contractions in the paragraph above that are made from the word *not*.

_____   _____

 **Ideas**   Use the "5 Ws" to make your writing interesting.
Tell *who, what, when, where,* and *why.*

A. Write the missing details to tell *who, what, when, where,* or *why.*

Details		
to Danville Junior High	fifty years ago	cellphone
my grandma Beth	it was against the rules	at 4:00
her friend Selma	in Selma's locker	skirt

When _____ went to school,
(who)

some things were different. It was _____
(when)

_____. Grandma went _____
(where)

_____. She wore a _____ or dress every day.
(what)

That's because _____
(why)

for girls to wear pants. Also, she did not have a _____
(what)

_____. It was not invented yet. So if she wanted to

send _____ a message, she had to put
(who)

a note _____. They often walked
(where)

home together after school _____. Grandma says
(when)

it's hard to believe how much has changed.

B. Read each pair of words. Write their contractions. Then circle
those contractions in the paragraph.

that + is = _____   it + is = _____

Name: _____

 **Ideas**   Use the "5 Ws"—*who, what, when, where,* and *why*— to help you plan your writing.

Think back to your first day of school this year. What details can you remember about it? Fill in the chart.

The First Day of School

Who was there:	
What you did:	
When it took place:	
Where things happened:	
Why you liked or didn't like it:	

DAY 1

Read the rule aloud, and review the concept of details. Say: *When you add details, you tell more about your topic. Strong details keep your reader interested in what you're saying.* Then guide students through the activities.

- **Activity A:** Read aloud the paragraph. Ask: *What is the topic?* (Emma's guinea pig) Then reread the first sentence. Ask: *Is that a detail?* (no) Read the third sentence. Ask: *Is that a detail?* (yes) Have students complete the activity.

- **Activity B:** Read Anna's sentences. Say: *I see that Spot has spots, so that's a detail. What other details do you see?* Have students write their answers.

- **Activity C (Convention):** Ask: *What punctuation mark always goes at the end of a question?* (question mark) Say: *When you write, be sure to end every question with a question mark.* Point out that the paragraphs in Activities A and B both contain questions. Have students find and circle the question marks.

DAY 2

Ask: *What are the five senses?* (sight, sound, touch, taste, smell) Say: *Sensory details describe how something looks, sounds, feels, tastes, or smells.* Read the rule aloud. Then guide students through the activities.

- **Activity A:** Say: *A riddle describes something by giving clues. You try to guess what the writer is describing.* Read aloud the first sentence. Ask: *Are* **soft** *and* **white** *sensory details?* (yes) Continue reading the riddle, pausing after each sentence for students to underline the sensory details.

- **Activity B:** Review the story of "Little Red Riding Hood." Then choose one of the characters and model thinking of clues about him or her. Say: *The Big Bad Wolf has big eyes, so that could be a clue.* Then have students write their riddles. When they are finished, invite students to read their riddles and have other students guess the answer.

- **Activity C (Convention):** Read aloud the exclamation. Ask: *How can we rearrange the words in this sentence to form a question?* Have students write their answers.

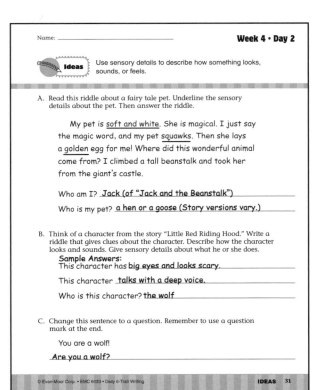

Name: _____ Week 4 • Day 1

Ideas   Choose strong details to interest your reader.

A. Read the paragraph about Emma's pet. Underline the details.

    Do you know what a guinea pig is? A guinea pig isn't really a pig. It <u>is a rodent,</u> just like hamsters and rats. What is a guinea pig like? My guinea pig <u>Isabelle is a small, gentle pet.</u> She <u>lets me hold her and brush her fur.</u>

B. Read what Anna wrote about her pet. She needs to add more details. Look at the picture and list three details she could add.

    Do you like dogs? I do. My dog Spot is three years old. We got him when he was a puppy. He is a fun pet to have.

Details:

1. <u>Sample Answers: He plays ball.</u>
2. <u>He shakes hands.</u>
3. <u>He eats dog biscuits.</u>

C. Circle the question marks in the paragraphs above.

Name: _____ Week 4 • Day 2

Ideas   Use sensory details to describe how something looks, sounds, or feels.

A. Read this riddle about a fairy tale pet. Underline the sensory details about the pet. Then answer the riddle.

    My pet is <u>soft and white.</u> She is magical. I just say the magic word, and my pet <u>squawks.</u> Then she lays a <u>golden</u> egg for me! Where did this wonderful animal come from? I climbed a tall beanstalk and took her from the giant's castle.

Who am I? <u>Jack (of "Jack and the Beanstalk")</u>

Who is my pet? <u>a hen or a goose (Story versions vary.)</u>

B. Think of a character from the story "Little Red Riding Hood." Write a riddle that gives clues about the character. Describe how the character looks and sounds. Give sensory details about what he or she does.
Sample Answers:
This character has <u>big eyes and looks scary.</u>

This character <u>talks with a deep voice.</u>

Who is this character? <u>the wolf</u>

C. Change this sentence to a question. Remember to use a question mark at the end.

    You are a wolf!

<u>Are you a wolf?</u>

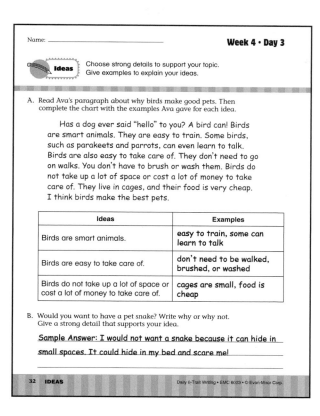

Name: _____

Ideas Choose strong details to support your topic.
Give examples to explain your ideas.

A. Read Ava's paragraph about why birds make good pets. Then
   complete the chart with the examples Ava gave for each idea.

  Has a dog ever said "hello" to you? A bird can! Birds
are smart animals. They are easy to train. Some birds,
such as parakeets and parrots, can even learn to talk.
Birds are also easy to take care of. They don't need to go
on walks. You don't have to brush or wash them. Birds do
not take up a lot of space or cost a lot of money to take
care of. They live in cages, and their food is very cheap.
I think birds make the best pets.

Ideas	Examples
Birds are smart animals.	easy to train, some can learn to talk
Birds are easy to take care of.	don't need to be walked, brushed, or washed
Birds do not take up a lot of space or cost a lot of money to take care of.	cages are small, food is cheap

B. Would you want to have a pet snake? Write why or why not.
   Give a strong detail that supports your idea.

  Sample Answer: I would not want a snake because it can hide in

  small spaces. It could hide in my bed and scare me!

32 IDEAS   Daily 6-Trait Writing • EMC 6023 • © Evan-Moor Corp.

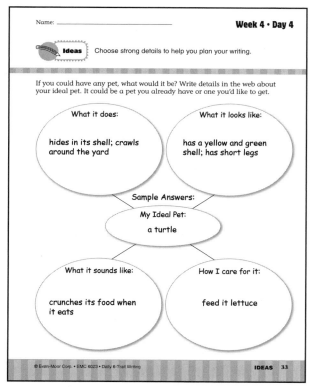

Name: _____   Week 4 · Day 4

Ideas Choose strong details to help you plan your writing.

If you could have any pet, what would it be? Write details in the web about
your ideal pet. It could be a pet you already have or one you'd like to get.

What it does:
hides in its shell; crawls around the yard

What it looks like:
has a yellow and green shell; has short legs

Sample Answers:

My Ideal Pet:
a turtle

What it sounds like:
crunches its food when it eats

How I care for it:
feed it lettuce

© Evan-Moor Corp. • EMC 6023 • Daily 6-Trait Writing   IDEAS 33

DAY 3

Read the rule aloud. Review the definition of **topic**.
(main idea, or what the writing is mainly about) Say:
*Details can help you make your point or support your
opinion.* Then guide students through the activities.

- **Activity A:** Have students read the paragraph.
  Then read aloud the first idea in the chart. Say:
  Ava thinks that birds are smart. Ask: *What details
  does she give about birds to provide examples of how
  birds are smart?* (birds are easy to train and can
  learn to talk) Have students write the examples
  in the top right-hand column. Repeat the process
  for ideas 2 and 3.

- **Activity B:** Briefly discuss why someone would
  or would not want a snake for a pet. Then have
  students write their responses. Invite volunteers
  to share their sentences with the class.

DAY 4

Review the rule. Guide students through the activity.

- Say: *This week, we've read a lot about pets.* Ask:
  What kind of pet would you want? Help students
  brainstorm details about pets by asking: *What
  would the animal do? What would it look and sound
  like? How would you care for it?* Encourage students
  to think outside the realm of traditional house
  pets, such as farm animals, jungle animals,
  imaginary animals, etc. They may also write
  about a pet they already have.

- Have students write their chosen animal in the
  center of the web. Then have them complete the
  web. Remind students to give specific examples
  and sensory details to support their ideas.

DAY 5 *Writing Prompt*

- *Write a paragraph that describes your ideal pet.
  Use the details you wrote on Day 4, but don't give
  away what kind of animal it is! At the end of your
  paragraph, write "What is it?" and let your reader
  guess the animal.*

- *Be sure to use a question mark at the end of the
  question.*

 **Ideas** Choose strong details to interest your reader.

A. Read the paragraph about Emma's pet.
   Underline the details.

> Do you know what a guinea pig is? A guinea pig isn't really a pig. It is a rodent, just like hamsters and rats. What is a guinea pig like? My guinea pig Isabelle is a small, gentle pet. She lets me hold her and brush her fur.

B. Read what Anna wrote about her pet. She needs to add more details. Look at the picture and list three details she could add.

> Do you like dogs? I do. My dog Spot is three years old. We got him when he was a puppy. He is a fun pet to have.

Details:

1. _____

2. _____

3. _____

C. Circle the question marks in the paragraphs above.

Name: _____

 **Ideas**   Use sensory details to describe how something looks, sounds, or feels.

A. Read this riddle about a fairy tale pet. Underline the sensory details about the pet. Then answer the riddle.

> My pet is soft and white. She is magical. I just say the magic word, and my pet squawks. Then she lays a golden egg for me! Where did this wonderful animal come from? I climbed a tall beanstalk and took her from the giant's castle.

Who am I? _____

Who is my pet? _____

B. Think of a character from the story "Little Red Riding Hood." Write a riddle that gives clues about the character. Describe how the character looks and sounds. Give sensory details about what he or she does.

This character has _____

This character _____

Who is this character? _____

C. Change this sentence to a question. Remember to use a question mark at the end.

You are a wolf!

_____

Ideas

Choose strong details to support your topic.
Give examples to explain your ideas.

A. Read Ava's paragraph about why birds make good pets. Then complete the chart with the examples Ava gave for each idea.

Has a dog ever said "hello" to you? A bird can! Birds are smart animals. They are easy to train. Some birds, such as parakeets and parrots, can even learn to talk. Birds are also easy to take care of. They don't need to go on walks. You don't have to brush or wash them. Birds do not take up a lot of space or cost a lot of money to take care of. They live in cages, and their food is very cheap. I think birds make the best pets.

Ideas	Examples
Birds are smart animals.	
Birds are easy to take care of.	
Birds do not take up a lot of space or cost a lot of money to take care of.	

B. Would you want to have a pet snake? Write why or why not. Give a strong detail that supports your idea.

_____

_____

_____

 **Ideas**   Choose strong details to help you plan your writing.

If you could have any pet, what would it be? Write details in the web about your ideal pet. It could be a pet you already have or one you'd like to get.

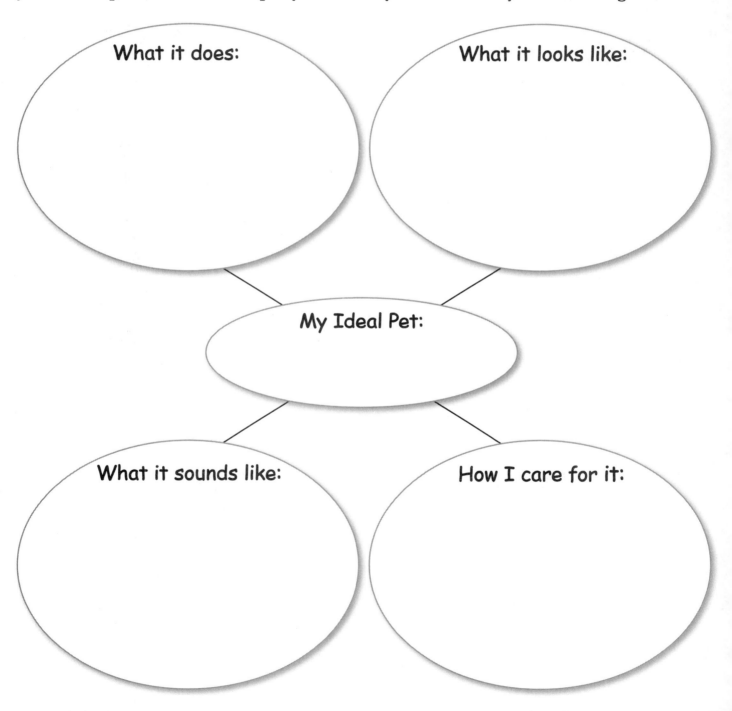

What it does:

What it looks like:

My Ideal Pet:

What it sounds like:

How I care for it:

DAY 1

Read the rule aloud. Then say: *When you write, it's important that all of your details stick to your topic. If you don't stick to your topic, your reader may become confused.* Read the following and ask students to listen for a detail that doesn't stick to the topic: *A lake is a body of water. It is surrounded on all sides by land. Collecting rocks is fun. Lakes can be small or large.* Ask: *Which detail doesn't belong?* (collecting rocks, because it is not about a lake) Then guide students through the activities.

- **Activity A:** Have students look at the first picture and read each sentence below it. Ask: *What is the topic of the picture?* (a family packing the car for a trip) *Which sentence does not stick to that topic?* ("We had pizza...") Repeat for the remaining pictures and sentences.

- **Activity B (Convention):** Write your city and state on the board, modeling the use of a comma between the city and state (or province). Then read the place names in the activity. Help students identify the city and state in each one. Have students complete the activity independently.

DAY 2

Read the rule aloud. Then guide students through the activities.

- **Activity A:** Read the letter aloud. Ask: *What is Glenn's topic?* (the area where he lives) Have students name the details that stick to that topic. Then reread the last sentence of the letter. Ask: *Does this sentence stick to the topic?* (no) Say: *Books about mummies don't have anything to do with where Glenn lives, so this sentence should be crossed out.* Then have students find and cross out the other irrelevant details. Review the answers as a class.

- **Activity B (Convention):** Ask: *What are two things you can say about where we live?* Encourage students to think of landforms, climate, and other important features of your area. Then have students write their sentences on their own or in pairs.

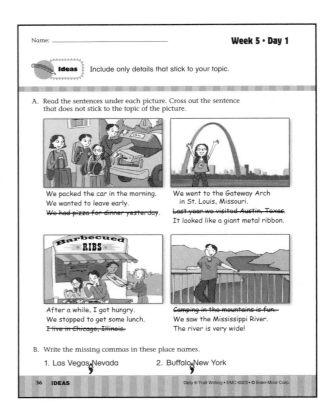

Name: _____ **Week 5 • Day 1**

Ideas Include only details that stick to your topic.

A. Read the sentences under each picture. Cross out the sentence that does not stick to the topic of the picture.

We packed the car in the morning. We wanted to leave early. ~~We had pizza for dinner yesterday.~~

We went to the Gateway Arch in St. Louis, Missouri. ~~Last year we visited Austin, Texas.~~ It looked like a giant metal ribbon.

After a while, I got hungry. We stopped to get some lunch. ~~I live in Chicago, Illinois.~~

~~Camping in the mountains is fun.~~ We saw the Mississippi River. The river is very wide!

B. Write the missing commas in these place names.

1. Las Vegas, Nevada   2. Buffalo, New York

36 IDEAS   Daily 6-Trait Writing • EMC 6023 • © Evan-Moor Corp.

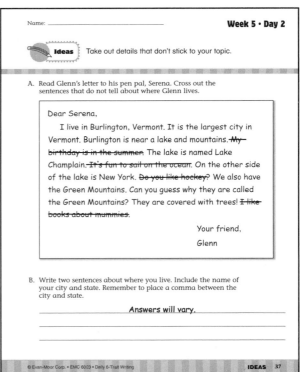

Name: _____ **Week 5 • Day 2**

Ideas Take out details that don't stick to your topic.

A. Read Glenn's letter to his pen pal, Serena. Cross out the sentences that do not tell about where Glenn lives.

Dear Serena,

    I live in Burlington, Vermont. It is the largest city in Vermont. Burlington is near a lake and mountains. ~~My birthday is in the summer.~~ The lake is named Lake Champlain. ~~It's fun to sail on the ocean.~~ On the other side of the lake is New York. ~~Do you like hockey?~~ We also have the Green Mountains. Can you guess why they are called the Green Mountains? They are covered with trees! ~~I like books about mummies.~~

                    Your friend,
                    Glenn

B. Write two sentences about where you live. Include the name of your city and state. Remember to place a comma between the city and state.

                    Answers will vary.
_____
_____

© Evan-Moor Corp. • EMC 6023 • Daily 6-Trait Writing   **IDEAS** 37

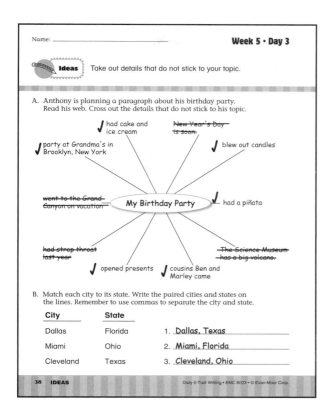

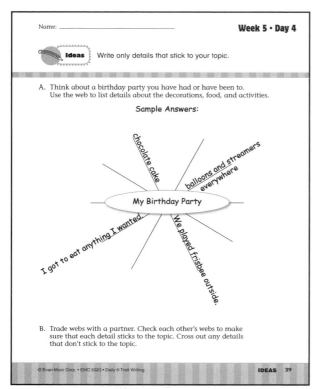

Read the rule aloud. Then guide students through the activities.

- **Activity A:** Have students read through the web. Then ask: *What is Anthony's topic?* (his birthday party) Read each detail and have students make a check next to it if it is about Anthony's birthday. Have them cross out the remaining details.

- **Activity B (Convention):** If necessary, use a U.S. map to help students pair the cities and states. Then have students complete the activity.

Read the rule aloud. Then guide students through the activities.

- **Activity A:** Say: *Using a web can help you plan what details to include in your writing in order to stick to your topic.* Help students brainstorm details related to a party they have been to. For example, ask: *Where and when was it? What did the decorations look like? What did you eat or drink? Did you play games? Who was there?* Have students fill out their webs. Circulate to assist as needed.

- **Activity B:** Have students work in pairs to check each other's webs. After students have crossed out details that don't stick to the topic, invite students to point out any details in their partner's webs that could be more specific. Encourage students to make those revisions.

DAY 5 *Writing Prompt*

- *Write a description of a birthday party, using the details you wrote on Day 4. Make sure your details stick to your topic.*

- *Write the name of the city and state (or province) where the party took place. Be sure to use a comma to separate the place names.*

 **Ideas** Include only details that stick to your topic.

A. Read the sentences under each picture. Cross out the sentence that does not stick to the topic of the picture.

We packed the car in the morning.
We wanted to leave early.
We had pizza for dinner yesterday.

We went to the Gateway Arch
   in St. Louis, Missouri.
Last year we visited Austin, Texas.
It looked like a giant metal ribbon.

After a while, I got hungry.
We stopped to get some lunch.
I live in Chicago, Illinois.

Camping in the mountains is fun.
We saw the Mississippi River.
The river is very wide!

B. Write the missing commas in these place names.

   1. Las Vegas Nevada   2. Buffalo New York

Ideas Take out details that don't stick to your topic.

A. Read Glenn's letter to his pen pal, Serena. Cross out the sentences that do not tell about where Glenn lives.

> Dear Serena,
>
> I live in Burlington, Vermont. It is the largest city in Vermont. Burlington is near a lake and mountains. My birthday is in the summer. The lake is named Lake Champlain. It's fun to sail on the ocean. On the other side of the lake is New York. Do you like hockey? We also have the Green Mountains. Can you guess why they are called the Green Mountains? They are covered with trees! I like books about mummies.
>
> Your friend,
>
> Glenn

B. Write two sentences about where you live. Include the name of your city and state. Remember to place a comma between the city and state.

_____

_____

_____

Ideas : Take out details that do not stick to your topic.

A. Anthony is planning a paragraph about his birthday party.
   Read his web. Cross out the details that do not stick to his topic.

had cake and
ice cream

New Year's Day
is soon.

party at Grandma's in
Brooklyn, New York

blew out candles

went to the Grand
Canyon on vacation

My Birthday Party

had a piñata

had strep throat
last year

The Science Museum
has a big volcano.

opened presents

cousins Ben and
Marley came

B. Match each city to its state. Write the paired cities and states on
   the lines. Remember to use commas to separate the city and state.

City	State	
Dallas	Florida	1. _____
Miami	Ohio	2. _____
Cleveland	Texas	3. _____

Ideas Write only details that stick to your topic.

A. Think about a birthday party you have had or have been to.
   Use the web to list details about the decorations, food, and activities.

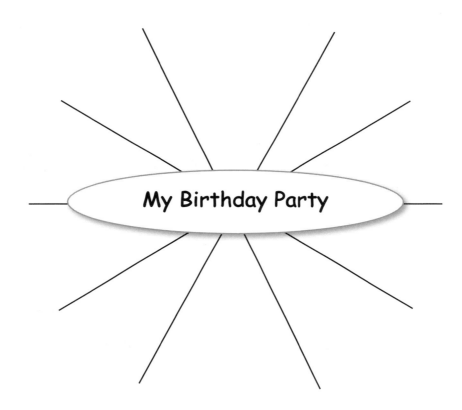

My Birthday Party

B. Trade webs with a partner. Check each other's webs to make
   sure that each detail sticks to the topic. Cross out any details
   that don't stick to the topic.

ORGANIZATION
Beginning, Middle, and End

Refer to pages 6 and 7 to introduce or review the writing trait.

DAY 1

Read the rule aloud. Than ask: *Which of these beginnings makes you want to read more of the story?: 1) "Grandma isn't feeling well today. Please be a dear and bring her these cupcakes," Mother said to Red. or 2) One day, Little Red Riding Hood went to her grandma's house.* (1) Say: *Using a quotation is one way to grab your reader's interest. It immediately gives details about the story and characters. What did the quotation from "Little Red Riding Hood" reveal?* (Grandma was ill; Red was bringing her cupcakes.) Then say: *There are other good ways to begin a story.* Call students' attention to the methods listed in Activity A and read them aloud. Then guide students through the activities.

- **Activity A:** Have a student read the two choices in item 1. Ask: *Which beginning grabs your attention more?* (b) Then ask: *What method was used to grab your attention?* (creating a feeling of mystery by using the words "something was different") Repeat the process for each story beginning.

- **Activity B (Convention):** Review the definition of an exclamation. (A sentence that shows strong feeling.) Point out that an exclamation can also be a sound word, such as **Pop! Crash!** or **Bang!** Have students find and circle the exclamation points in Activity A.

DAY 2

Read the rule aloud. Then say: *For a story to be good, it has to have something interesting happen in the middle of it. It also has events that make sense and are in the right order.* Then guide students through the activity.

- Have students follow along as you read the beginning and ending of the story. Then say: *What could have happened in the middle to make Ben and Mauler become friends?* Brainstorm with students different events that could have occurred. Remind students that the middle must make sense with the beginning and ending.

- Have students draw and write their middles. Remind them to use at least one exclamation. Then have volunteers share their completed stories.

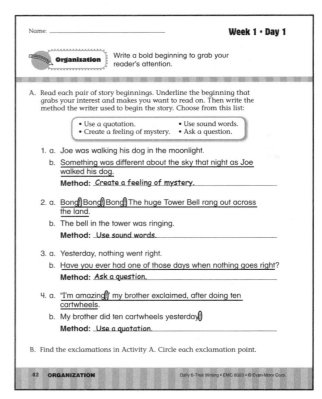

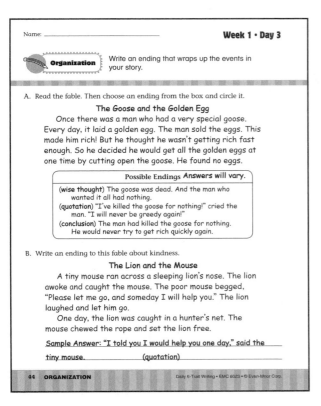

Name: _____

Week 1 • Day 3

Organization — Write an ending that wraps up the events in your story.

A. Read the fable. Then choose an ending from the box and circle it.

The Goose and the Golden Egg

Once there was a man who had a very special goose. Every day, it laid a golden egg. The man sold the eggs. This made him rich! But he thought he wasn't getting rich fast enough. So he decided he would get all the golden eggs at one time by cutting open the goose. He found no eggs.

Possible Endings Answers will vary.

(wise thought) The goose was dead. And the man who wanted it all had nothing.
(quotation) "I've killed the goose for nothing!" cried the man. "I will never be greedy again!"
(conclusion) The man had killed the goose for nothing. He would never try to get rich quickly again.

B. Write an ending to this fable about kindness.

The Lion and the Mouse

A tiny mouse ran across a sleeping lion's nose. The lion awoke and caught the mouse. The poor mouse begged, "Please let me go, and someday I will help you." The lion laughed and let him go.

One day, the lion was caught in a hunter's net. The mouse chewed the rope and set the lion free.

Sample Answer: "I told you I would help you one day," said the

tiny mouse. (quotation)

44   ORGANIZATION   Daily 6-Trait Writing • EMC 6023 • © Evan-Moor Corp.

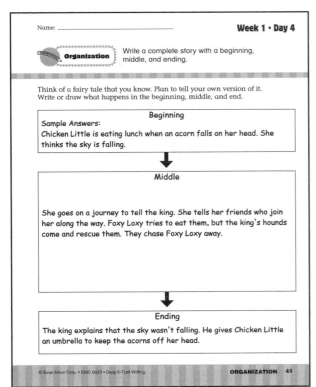

Name: _____

Week 1 • Day 4

Organization — Write a complete story with a beginning, middle, and ending.

Think of a fairy tale that you know. Plan to tell your own version of it. Write or draw what happens in the beginning, middle, and end.

Beginning
Sample Answers:
Chicken Little is eating lunch when an acorn falls on her head. She thinks the sky is falling.

Middle

She goes on a journey to tell the king. She tells her friends who join her along the way. Foxy Loxy tries to eat them, but the king's hounds come and rescue them. They chase Foxy Loxy away.

Ending
The king explains that the sky wasn't falling. He gives Chicken Little an umbrella to keep the acorns off her head.

© Evan-Moor Corp. • EMC 6023 • Daily 6-Trait Writing   ORGANIZATION   45

DAY 3

Read the rule aloud. Say: *It's not enough to write the words "the end." You have to tie up everything that has happened in the beginning and middle.* Then guide students through the activities.

- **Activity A:** Read the story aloud. Say: *There are many ways to end this story.* Read the possible endings aloud. Then point out that each of them says about the same thing, but in a different way. Ask: *Which ending would you use for this story? Why?*

- **Activity B:** Read the story aloud. Ask: *What could happen at the end of this story?* (e.g., The lion thanks the mouse.) Remind students that the ending must make sense with the beginning and middle. Have them choose one type of ending from Activity A to use, and then write their own endings. Ask volunteers to share their endings and identify the type they chose.

DAY 4

Read the rule aloud. Then guide students through the activity.

- Brainstorm with students different fairy tales they know. Then have them choose one to rewrite in their own words. You may wish students who have chosen the same fairy tale to work together.

- Have students jot down ideas for an attention-getting beginning, using the methods from Day 1. Then have them write or draw the middle events in the boxes. Finally, have students write ideas for an ending that uses one of the types of endings from Day 3. Offer help as necessary. Ask volunteers to share their ideas.

DAY 5 *Writing Prompt*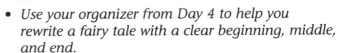

- *Use your organizer from Day 4 to help you rewrite a fairy tale with a clear beginning, middle, and end.*

- *Use an exclamation in your story. Be sure to end it with an exclamation point.*

 **Organization**   Write a bold beginning to grab your reader's attention.

A. Read each pair of story beginnings. Underline the beginning that grabs your interest and makes you want to read on. Then write the method the writer used to begin the story. Choose from this list:

> • Use a quotation.   • Use sound words.
> • Create a feeling of mystery.   • Ask a question.

1. a. Joe was walking his dog in the moonlight.

    b. Something was different about the sky that night as Joe walked his dog.

    Method: _____

2. a. Bong! Bong! Bong! The huge Tower Bell rang out across the land.

    b. The bell in the tower was ringing.

    Method: _____

3. a. Yesterday, nothing went right.

    b. Have you ever had one of those days when nothing goes right?

    Method: _____

4. a. "I'm amazing!" my brother exclaimed, after doing ten cartwheels.

    b. My brother did ten cartwheels yesterday!

    Method: _____

B. Find the exclamations in Activity A. Circle each exclamation point.

 **Organization** Write a middle that is interesting and makes sense between the beginning and ending.

Read the beginning and ending of this story. Draw and write what happens in the middle. Make it exciting! Use at least one exclamation.

Mean Mauler and Me

| The bell rang at 3 o'clock. Everyone but Ben cheered. He had to walk home past Mr. Warren's place. | Mr. Warren had a dog named Mauler. Some kids said Mauler was part wolf. Every time Ben walked by Mr. Warren's house, Mauler chased him down the street. | Ben slowly trudged home. When he got near Mr. Warren's house, he darted behind a lamppost. Then he dashed under a bush. Suddenly, Ben heard a deep growl. |

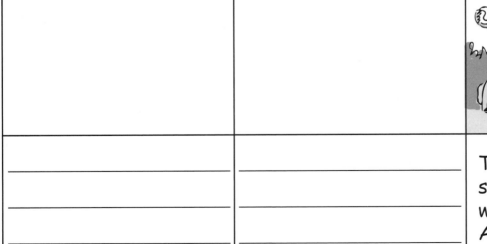 

| | | The next day after school, Ben couldn't wait to see Mauler. And Mauler couldn't wait to see him! |

Organization   Write an ending that wraps up the events in your story.

A. Read the fable. Then choose an ending from the box and circle it.

The Goose and the Golden Egg

Once there was a man who had a very special goose. Every day, it laid a golden egg. The man sold the eggs. This made him rich! But he thought he wasn't getting rich fast enough. So he decided he would get all the golden eggs at one time by cutting open the goose. He found no eggs.

Possible Endings

(wise thought) The goose was dead. And the man who wanted it all had nothing.

(quotation) "I've killed the goose for nothing!" cried the man. "I will never be greedy again!"

(conclusion) The man had killed the goose for nothing. He would never try to get rich quickly again.

B. Write an ending to this fable about kindness.

The Lion and the Mouse

A tiny mouse ran across a sleeping lion's nose. The lion awoke and caught the mouse. The poor mouse begged, "Please let me go, and someday I will help you." The lion laughed and let him go.

One day, the lion was caught in a hunter's net. The mouse chewed the rope and set the lion free.

_____

_____

 **Organization**   Write a complete story with a beginning, middle, and ending.

Think of a fairy tale that you know. Plan to tell your own version of it. Write or draw what happens in the beginning, middle, and end.

Beginning

Middle

Ending

DAY 1

Read the rule aloud. Say: *When you write, it is important to put things in the right order so the writing makes sense to your reader. Using order words such as **first, next, then, now,** and **finally** can also help the reader follow along.* Then guide students through the activities.

- **Activity A:** Have students underline the order words in the directions. Then read and discuss the picture sequence for "How to Make a Wind Vane." Look at picture 1 and ask: *What does this picture tell us to do?* (cut out the arrow shapes) Have students find the sentence that describes this below. ("cut out an arrow's point and tail") Have them write number 1 in front of it. Then ask: *Which order word fits in the sentence?* (**First**) Have them write the word. Continue with the remaining steps.

- **Activity B:** Explain that a comma is usually placed after introductory order words such as **first, next,** etc., to make the sentence easier to understand. Have students find and circle the commas.

DAY 2

Read the rule aloud. Ask: *When you are writing directions, what would happen if you didn't write the steps in order?* (no one could follow the directions) Then guide students through the activities.

- **Activity A:** Have students read the phrases in the box. Point out that each one begins with an order word or phrase. Then read aloud "Making a Fog Picture." Ask: *Which phrase belongs in the first blank?* ("To begin, cut out") *Why?* (The phrase **To begin** indicates it should be first.) Guide students through the rest of the paragraph.

- **Activity B (Convention):** Read the sentences aloud, pausing after each order word. Then have students complete the activity independently.

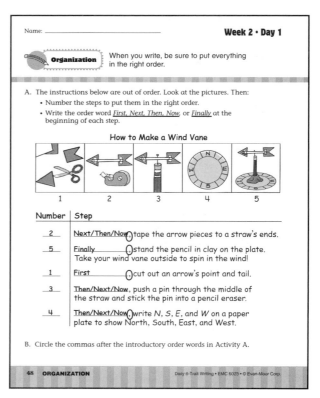

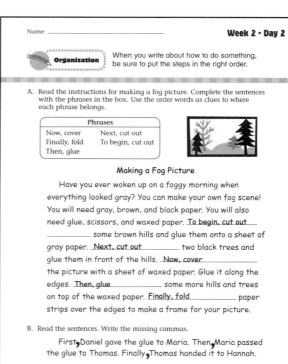

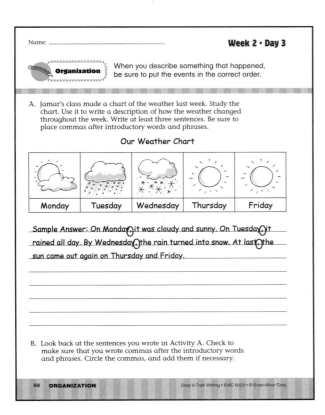

Read the rule aloud. Ask: *If you didn't tell about events in order, would your reader understand what happened?* (no) Then guide students through the activities.

- **Activity A:** Help students interpret the chart. For example, ask: *What does the chart tell about the weather on Monday? How did it change on Tuesday?*

  Say: *Think about how the weather changed throughout the week. How could you describe those changes? How can you make your writing clear for the reader?* Model using the days of the week to form introductory words or phrases with commas after them. (e.g., **On Tuesday,** or **By Wednesday,**)

  Have students write their descriptions. Remind them to write about the days of the week in order. When finished, invite students to read their descriptions aloud.

- **Activity B:** Have students check their sentences for commas after introductory words and phrases. Circulate to offer assistance as needed.

Review the rule. Guide students through the activity.

- Say: *Imagine that we had a crazy weather day. For example, what would happen if you were eating lunch outside in the sunshine and it began to snow? What if you made a snowman on the playground, but it melted into a huge puddle before your very eyes? What if the wind began to blow and the puddle froze into a skating pond? What if you were dressed for rain, but the sun got so hot it could roast a marshmallow?*

- Have students brainstorm other unusual "what ifs" before jotting words and ideas onto their chart. If necessary, model how to write the ideas on the chart, using the sample answers on the reduced page to the left.

- *Write about a day when the weather was all mixed up! Use your ideas from the chart on Day 4.*

- *Be sure to write commas after introductory words and phrases.*

 **Organization** When you write, be sure to put everything in the right order.

A. The instructions below are out of order. Look at the pictures. Then:

- Number the steps to put them in the right order.
- Write the order word *First, Next, Then, Now,* or *Finally* at the beginning of each step.

How to Make a Wind Vane

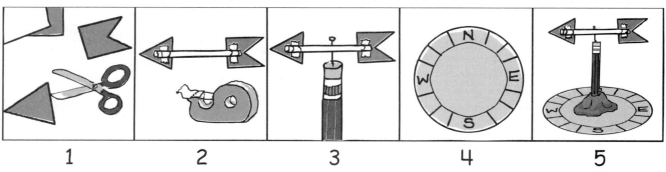

Number	Step
_____	_____, tape the arrow pieces to a straw's ends.
_____	_____, stand the pencil in clay on the plate. Take your wind vane outside to spin in the wind!
_____	_____, cut out an arrow's point and tail.
_____	_____, push a pin through the middle of the straw and stick the pin into a pencil eraser.
_____	_____, write *N, S, E,* and *W* on a paper plate to show North, South, East, and West.

B. Circle the commas after the introductory order words in Activity A.

 **Organization**   When you write about how to do something, be sure to put the steps in the right order.

A. Read the instructions for making a fog picture. Complete the sentences with the phrases in the box. Use the order words as clues to where each phrase belongs.

Phrases	
Now, cover	Next, cut out
Finally, fold	To begin, cut out
Then, glue	

Making a Fog Picture

Have you ever woken up on a foggy morning when everything looked gray? You can make your own fog scene! You will need gray, brown, and black paper. You will also need glue, scissors, and waxed paper. _____

_____ some brown hills and glue them onto a sheet of gray paper. _____ two black trees and glue them in front of the hills. _____ the picture with a sheet of waxed paper. Glue it along the edges. _____ some more hills and trees on top of the waxed paper. _____ paper strips over the edges to make a frame for your picture.

B. Read the sentences. Write the missing commas.

First Daniel gave the glue to Maria. Then Maria passed the glue to Thomas. Finally Thomas handed it to Hannah.

 **Organization**

When you describe something that happened, be sure to put the events in the correct order.

A. Jamar's class made a chart of the weather last week. Study the chart. Use it to write a description of how the weather changed throughout the week. Write at least three sentences. Be sure to place commas after introductory words and phrases.

Our Weather Chart

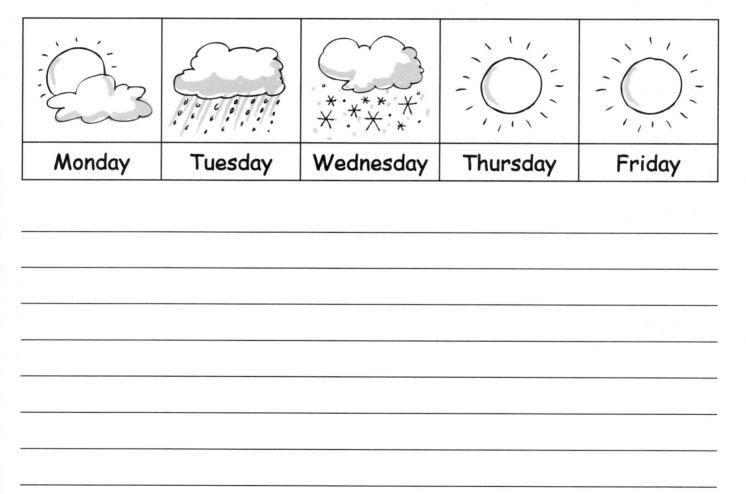

_____

_____

_____

_____

_____

_____

_____

_____

B. Look back at the sentences you wrote in Activity A. Check to make sure that you wrote commas after the introductory words and phrases. Circle the commas, and add them if necessary.

 **Organization**   When you describe something that happened, be sure to put the events in the correct order.

Imagine that you had a mixed-up weather day. It went from spring to summer to fall to winter, all in one day! What was your day like? How did the weather change your plans? Write your ideas on the chart.

A Mixed-up Weather Day

Time	Weather	Activity
Morning		
Lunchtime		
Afternoon		
After School		
Evening		

ORGANIZATION
Grouping Together Ideas and Details

DAY 1

Read the rule aloud. Then say: *Keeping our thoughts organized helps the reader follow what we write. Imagine a grocery store where the bananas, oranges, and apples were all mixed up. It would be confusing to shop there. That's why the fruit is usually sorted into baskets or bins. When we write, ideas are like the baskets, and details are like the fruit.* Then guide students through the activities.

- **Activity A:** Read the paragraph aloud. Have students underline the details. Then say: *Let's examine how Lani grouped her ideas and details.* Ask: *Where are all the details about English?* (together near the top of the paragraph) *Where are the details about Hawaiian?* (grouped together after the details about English) Say: *The grouping of her details shows the organization.*

- **Activity B (Convention):** Write **their, there,** and **they're** on the board. Say: *These words are homophones, or words that sound alike but have different spellings and meanings. **Their** means "belonging to them." **There** means "at that place." **They're** is a contraction of **they are.*** Have students complete the activity.

DAY 2

Read the rule aloud. Then write this sentence on the board: *Squanto helped the Pilgrims.* Ask students which of the following sentences should be grouped with it: *1) He showed them how to plant corn.* or *2) He was captured and taken to Spain.* (Sentence 1) Ask: *Why?* (Because it tells how Squanto helped.) Then guide students through the activity.

- Read the story aloud, noting the places where details are missing.

- Read aloud the details. Point out the word **There** in the second detail and ask: *Is this the correct spelling?* (no) *What should it be?* (**They're**) Have students fix the error.

- Ask: *Which detail belongs after the first sentence?* ("Those plants...") *Why? (It explains what the three plants are called and connects to the next sentence.)* Repeat the process for the remaining details. Then have a volunteer read the completed paragraph aloud.

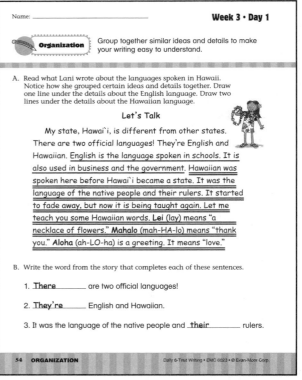

Name: _____ **Week 3 • Day 1**

Organization Group together similar ideas and details to make your writing easy to understand.

A. Read what Lani wrote about the languages spoken in Hawaii. Notice how she grouped certain ideas and details together. Draw one line under the details about the English language. Draw two lines under the details about the Hawaiian language.

Let's Talk

My state, Hawai`i, is different from other states. There are two official languages! They're English and Hawaiian. English is the language spoken in schools. It is also used in business and the government. Hawaiian was spoken here before Hawai`i became a state. It was the language of the native people and their rulers. It started to fade away, but now it is being taught again. Let me teach you some Hawaiian words. **Lei** (lay) means "a necklace of flowers." **Mahalo** (mah-HA-lo) means "thank you." **Aloha** (ah-LO-ha) is a greeting. It means "love."

B. Write the word from the story that completes each of these sentences.

1. __There_____ are two official languages!

2. __They're_____ English and Hawaiian.

3. It was the language of the native people and __their_____ rulers.

54 **ORGANIZATION** Daily 6-Trait Writing • EMC 6023 • © Evan-Moor Corp.

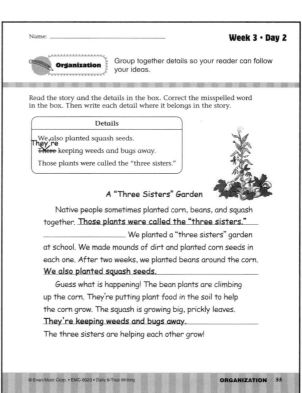

Name: _____ **Week 3 • Day 2**

Organization Group together details so your reader can follow your ideas.

Read the story and the details in the box. Correct the misspelled word in the box. Then write each detail where it belongs in the story.

Details

We also planted squash seeds.

~~There~~ They're keeping weeds and bugs away.

Those plants were called the "three sisters."

A "Three Sisters" Garden

Native people sometimes planted corn, beans, and squash together. Those plants were called the "three sisters." _____ We planted a "three sisters" garden at school. We made mounds of dirt and planted corn seeds in each one. After two weeks, we planted beans around the corn. We also planted squash seeds.

Guess what is happening! The bean plants are climbing up the corn. They're putting plant food in the soil to help the corn grow. The squash is growing big, prickly leaves. They're keeping weeds and bugs away.

The three sisters are helping each other grow!

© Evan-Moor Corp. • EMC 6023 • Daily 6-Trait Writing **ORGANIZATION** 55

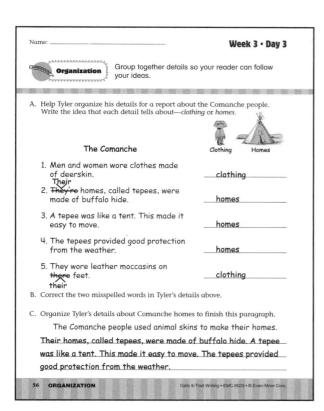

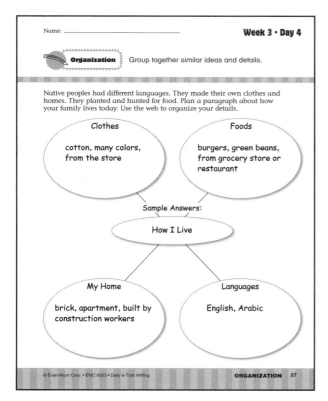

DAY 3

Review the rule. Then guide students through the activities.

- **Activity A:** After students examine the pictures, read the first detail and ask: *Is this detail about clothing or homes?* (clothing) Have students complete the rest of the activity independently. Go over the answers as a class.

- **Activity B (Convention):** Review the meanings of **their**, **there**, and **they're**. Remind students that these homophones are easy to mix up. Have students find and fix the incorrect homophones in Tyler's details.

- **Activity C:** Say: *Let's help Tyler write his paragraph. The topic sentence has already been written. Which sentence above might come next?* Decide as a class, or have students work independently to complete the activity.

DAY 4

Read the rule aloud. Then guide students to complete the activity.

- Invite students to think about how their lives compare with those of people long ago. (e.g., Native peoples made their own clothes and homes from plants and animals.) Ask: *What are your clothes made from? Where do you get them?* (e.g., cotton, from the store) *What foods do you eat? Where do you get them?* (e.g., hamburgers, from a store or restaurant) *What is your home like?* (e.g., apartment building, brick) *Is more than one language spoken at home?*

- After students have listed their ideas in the web, point out that the web has helped them group their details into categories, so writing an organized paragraph will be easy.

DAY 5 *Writing Prompt*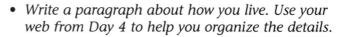

- *Write a paragraph about how you live. Use your web from Day 4 to help you organize the details.*

- *Be sure to use **their**, **there**, and **they're** correctly.*

Organization : Group together similar ideas and details to make your writing easy to understand.

A. Read what Lani wrote about the languages spoken in Hawaii. Notice how she grouped certain ideas and details together. Draw one line under the details about the English language. Draw two lines under the details about the Hawaiian language.

Let's Talk

My state, Hawai`i, is different from other states. There are two official languages! They're English and Hawaiian. English is the language spoken in schools. It is also used in business and the government. Hawaiian was spoken here before Hawai`i became a state. It was the language of the native people and their rulers. It started to fade away, but now it is being taught again. Let me teach you some Hawaiian words. **Lei** (lay) means "a necklace of flowers." **Mahalo** (mah-HA-lo) means "thank you." **Aloha** (ah-LO-ha) is a greeting. It means "love."

B. Write the word from the story that completes each of these sentences.

1. _____ are two official languages!

2. _____ English and Hawaiian.

3. It was the language of the native people and _____ rulers.

Organization Group together details so your reader can follow your ideas.

Read the story and the details in the box. Correct the misspelled word in the box. Then write each detail where it belongs in the story.

Details
We also planted squash seeds.
There keeping weeds and bugs away.
Those plants were called the "three sisters."

A "Three Sisters" Garden

Native people sometimes planted corn, beans, and squash together. _____

_____ We planted a "three sisters" garden at school. We made mounds of dirt and planted corn seeds in each one. After two weeks, we planted beans around the corn.

_____

Guess what is happening! The bean plants are climbing up the corn. They're putting plant food in the soil to help the corn grow. The squash is growing big, prickly leaves.

_____

The three sisters are helping each other grow!

 **Organization**   Group together details so your reader can follow your ideas.

A. Help Tyler organize his details for a report about the Comanche people. Write the idea that each detail tells about—*clothing* or *homes*.

The Comanche

Clothing   Homes

1. Men and women wore clothes made of deerskin.   _____

2. They're homes, called tepees, were made of buffalo hide.   _____

3. A tepee was like a tent. This made it easy to move.   _____

4. The tepees provided good protection from the weather.   _____

5. They wore leather moccasins on there feet.   _____

B. Correct the two misspelled words in Tyler's details above.

C. Organize Tyler's details about Comanche homes to finish this paragraph.

   The Comanche people used animal skins to make their homes.

_____

_____

_____

 **Organization**   Group together similar ideas and details.

Native peoples had different languages. They made their own clothes and homes. They planted and hunted for food. Plan a paragraph about how your family lives today. Use the web to organize your details.

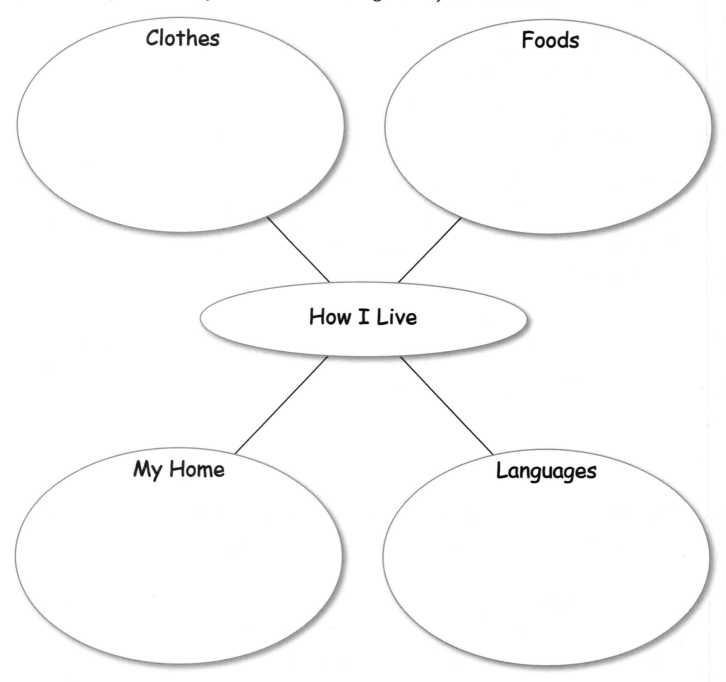

DAY 1

Read the rule aloud. Then guide students through the activities.

- **Activity A:** Explain that Faith Ringgold and Jerry Pinkney are two famous illustrators. (Students may be familiar with Ringgold's <u>Tar Beach</u> and Pinkney's <u>The Talking Eggs</u>.) Read the paragraph aloud. Ask: *Which sentences tell how the illustrators are alike?* (the first two) *What important word is in each sentence?* (**both**) Say: **Both** *is a signal word. It tells the reader that what follows is how the two are alike or different.*

- **Activity B:** Read the paragraph aloud. Point out the signal word **unlike**, which indicates that what follows is different. Ask: *How does the paragraph change after* **unlike**? (e.g., It tells how Pinkney is different.) Guide students to fill in the chart.

- **Activity C (Convention):** Say: *When writing, we need to underline the titles of books to make them stand out.* Point out the book titles in Activity A. Then have students complete Activity C.

DAY 2

Review the rule. Then guide students through the activities.

- **Activity A:** Remind students that a Venn diagram shows how two things are alike (where the circles overlap) and different (outer sections). Say: *A Venn diagram can help you organize your writing by showing you how to group details according to how two things are alike and different.* Discuss the contents of Sofia's diagram. Ask: *How are the two books alike?* (illustrator, main character, clothing and quilts) *How are they different?* (authors, publication date, setting)

- **Activity B:** Have students write their sentences independently. Encourage them to use a signal word, such as **both**. Ask volunteers to share their sentences.

- **Activity C:** Have students write their sentences independently. Remind students to underline the titles of books. Then have volunteers share their sentences.

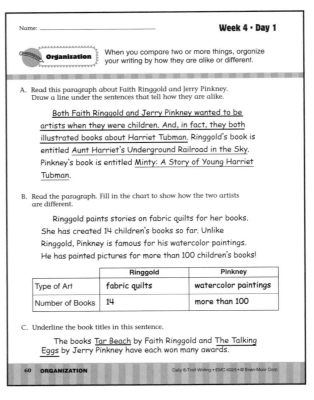

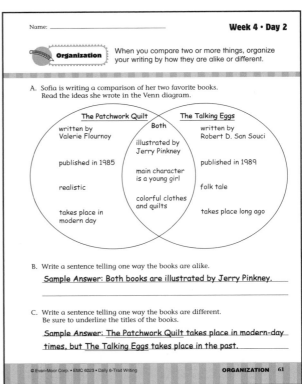

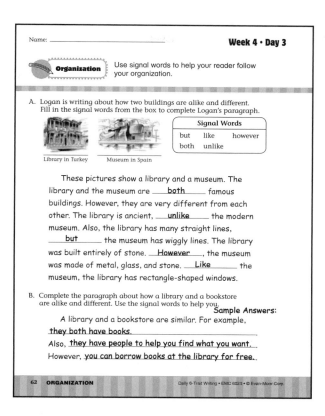

Name: _____   **Week 4 · Day 3**

Organization   Use signal words to help your reader follow your organization.

A. Logan is writing about how two buildings are alike and different. Fill in the signal words from the box to complete Logan's paragraph.

Library in Turkey   Museum in Spain

Signal Words

| but | like | however |
| both | unlike | |

These pictures show a library and a museum. The library and the museum are __both__ famous buildings. However, they are very different from each other. The library is ancient, __unlike__ the modern museum. Also, the library has many straight lines, __but__ the museum has wiggly lines. The library was built entirely of stone. __However__, the museum was made of metal, glass, and stone. __Like__ the museum, the library has rectangle-shaped windows.

B. Complete the paragraph about how a library and a bookstore are alike and different. Use the signal words to help you.
Sample Answers:
A library and a bookstore are similar. For example, __they both have books.__
Also, __they have people to help you find what you want.__
However, __you can borrow books at the library for free.__

62 **ORGANIZATION**   Daily 6-Trait Writing • EMC 6023 • © Evan-Moor Corp.

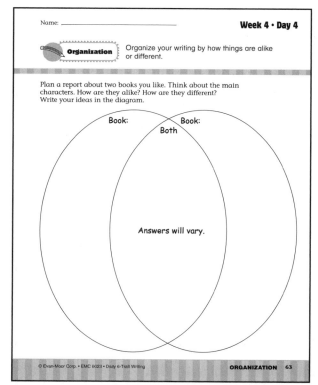

Name: _____   **Week 4 · Day 4**

Organization   Organize your writing by how things are alike or different.

Plan a report about two books you like. Think about the main characters. How are they alike? How are they different? Write your ideas in the diagram.

Book: _____   Book: _____

Both

Answers will vary.

© Evan-Moor Corp. • EMC 6023 • Daily 6-Trait Writing   **ORGANIZATION** 63

DAY 3

Read the rule aloud. Then review: *Signal words let the reader know what is coming up. The word **both** tells us that what follows is how two things are alike. The word **however** tells us that what follows is different from what came before.* Then guide students through the activities.

- **Activity A:** Read aloud the signal words and review their meanings. Then have students look at the pictures and read the paragraph together. Demonstrate how to determine which signal word fits in the first blank. For the second blank, say: *The library is ancient, **but** the modern library. Does that make sense?* (no) *The library is ancient, **unlike** the modern library. Does that make sense?* (yes) Have students complete the paragraph.

- **Activity B:** Read the first sentence and ask: *How are a library and bookstore alike?* (e.g., both have books) Point out **For example** and **Also**. Say: *These words are signal words. They tell us that we need to give examples of how the two places are alike.* Then point out **However**. Ask: *What should we do here?* (tell how the two places are different) Have students complete the activity.

DAY 4

Read the rule aloud. Then guide students through the activity.

- Either allow students to choose their own books to compare, or use two that you have read recently in class. You may also use two books from your classroom library and complete this activity as a group.

- Have students think about the characters in the books. Prompt students by asking: *What does each character look like? What does he or she do?*

DAY 5 *Writing Prompt*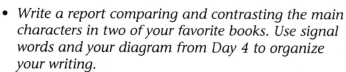

- *Write a report comparing and contrasting the main characters in two of your favorite books. Use signal words and your diagram from Day 4 to organize your writing.*

- *Be sure to underline the titles of the books.*

 **Organization**

When you compare two or more things, organize your writing by how they are alike or different.

A. Read this paragraph about Faith Ringgold and Jerry Pinkney. Draw a line under the sentences that tell how they are alike.

> Both Faith Ringgold and Jerry Pinkney wanted to be artists when they were children. And, in fact, they both illustrated books about Harriet Tubman. Ringgold's book is entitled <u>Aunt Harriet's Underground Railroad in the Sky</u>. Pinkney's book is entitled <u>Minty: A Story of Young Harriet Tubman</u>.

B. Read the paragraph. Fill in the chart to show how the two artists are different.

> Ringgold paints stories on fabric quilts for her books. She has created 14 children's books so far. Unlike Ringgold, Pinkney is famous for his watercolor paintings. He has painted pictures for more than 100 children's books!

	Ringgold	**Pinkney**
Type of Art		
Number of Books		

C. Underline the book titles in this sentence.

> The books Tar Beach by Faith Ringgold and The Talking Eggs by Jerry Pinkney have each won many awards.

 **Organization**   When you compare two or more things, organize your writing by how they are alike or different.

A. Sofia is writing a comparison of her two favorite books.
   Read the ideas she wrote in the Venn diagram.

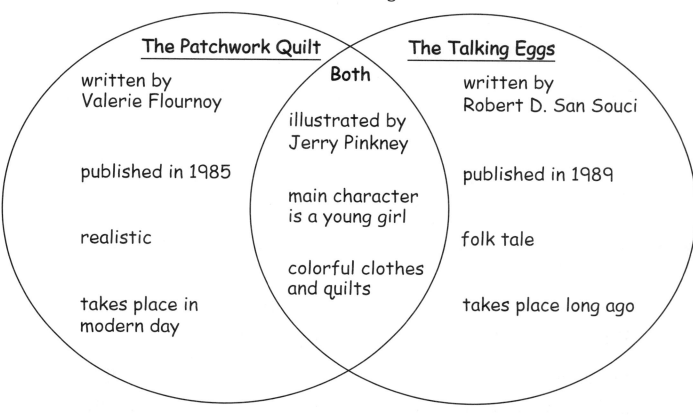

The Patchwork Quilt

written by
Valerie Flournoy

published in 1985

realistic

takes place in
modern day

Both

illustrated by
Jerry Pinkney

main character
is a young girl

colorful clothes
and quilts

The Talking Eggs

written by
Robert D. San Souci

published in 1989

folk tale

takes place long ago

B. Write a sentence telling one way the books are alike.

_____

_____

C. Write a sentence telling one way the books are different.
   Be sure to underline the titles of the books.

_____

_____

 **Organization**   Use signal words to help your reader follow your organization.

A. Logan is writing about how two buildings are alike and different. Fill in the signal words from the box to complete Logan's paragraph.

Library in Turkey   Museum in Spain

Signal Words		
but	like	however
both	unlike	

These pictures show a library and a museum. The library and the museum are _____ famous buildings. However, they are very different from each other. The library is ancient, _____ the modern museum. Also, the library has many straight lines, _____ the museum has wiggly lines. The library was built entirely of stone. _____, the museum was made of metal, glass, and stone. _____ the museum, the library has rectangle-shaped windows.

B. Complete the paragraph about how a library and a bookstore are alike and different. Use the signal words to help you.

A library and a bookstore are similar. For example,

_____.

Also, _____.

However, _____.

 **Organization**   Organize your writing by how things are alike or different.

Plan a report about two books you like. Think about the main characters. How are they alike? How are they different?
Write your ideas in the diagram.

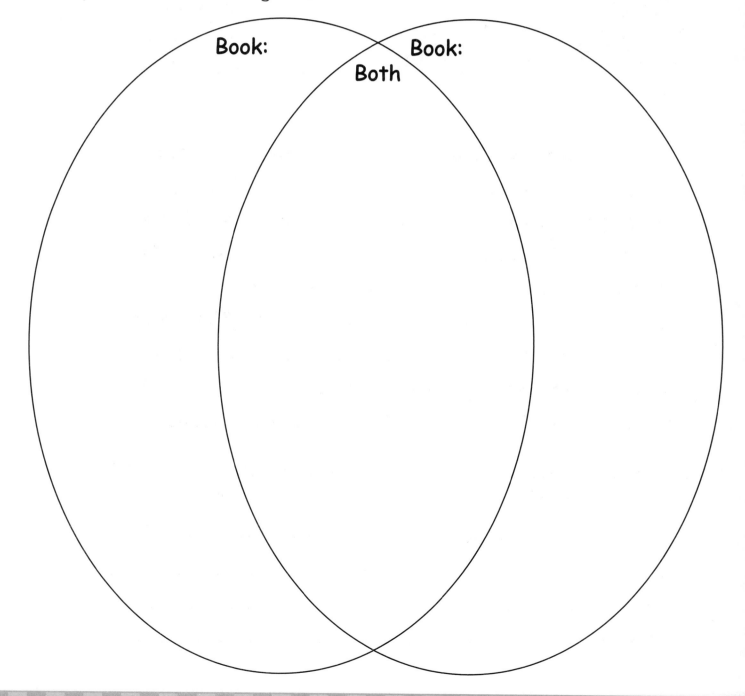

Book:

Both

Book:

DAY 1

Read the rule aloud. Say: *You must think carefully about which kind of organization is best for the topic and purpose of your writing.* Then guide students through the activities.

- **Activity A:** Have students read the two paragraphs. Ask: *Which explanation gives the steps in the right order?* (the second one) Point out how in the first paragraph, the details are grouped by what goes in the tank and how the water should be. However, that type of organization is not the best choice for a how-to paragraph. The steps must be in order.

- **Activity B:** Say: *Some words can be used at the beginning of a sentence to show order.* Help students identify the order words in the paragraph. (**First, Next, Then, Finally**)

- **Activity C (Convention):** Say: *Adjectives that end in **er** compare <u>two</u> people, places, or things. Adjectives with **est** compare <u>three or more</u>.* Then guide students through the activity, identifying the base word and ending of each adjective form.

DAY 2

Read the rule aloud. Then guide students through the activities.

- **Activity A:** Use the list to review the types of organization. Then read the first topic and say: *The words **How to** tell me this needs to be organized in steps. So I'll write **d** next to it.* Help students find clues in the remaining topics to determine how each one should be organized. (**Magic** means this must be fiction; **Smallest** and **Biggest** show that animals are being compared; **What's in** indicates a description of a place.)

- **Activity B:** Review the graphic organizers and their purposes. (comparing and contrasting; sequencing; grouping details) Have students complete the activity.

- **Activity C:** Have students find and circle the superlatives in Activity A. (**Smallest, Biggest**) Have volunteers share their sentences.

Name: _____   **Week 5 • Day 1**

Organization — The way you organize your writing depends on what you are writing about.

A. Makayla is writing about how to set up a new fish tank. Read the two explanations. Write an *X* next to the one that is organized more clearly.

☐ When you set up a fish tank, put plants and gravel in it. Put the fish in. But you have to make sure the tank is (clean). The water has to sit for three days before the fish can go in. Use a heater to make the water (warmer) My (older) brother helped me set up my (newest) fish tank.

☒ It's easy to set up a new fish tank. First, wash your new tank and put gravel in the bottom. Next, pour in water. Add plants, rocks, and caves. Then, put in a heater to warm up the water. Let the water sit for a few days. Finally, add your fish.

B. Write the four order words that were used in the second explanation.

____First____   ____Next____   ____Then____   ____Finally____

C. Write the form of each of these adjectives that were used in the first explanation. Find and circle the words in the paragraph.

1. new, newer, ___newest___

2. old, ___older___, oldest

3. ___clean___, cleaner, cleanest

4. warm, ___warmer___, warmest

Name: _____   **Week 5 • Day 2**

Organization — Choose the best way to organize your writing to fit your topic and purpose.

A. Read the ways to organize different types of writing. Then read each topic. Write the letter of the best way to organize the topic.

Ways to Organize
a. **Compare and Contrast:** Group things by how they are alike and different.
b. **Tell a Story:** Write a beginning, middle, and ending.
c. **Describe:** Group ideas and details together.
d. **Explain How:** Put steps in the right order.

Topics

How to Clean a Fish Tank __d__

The Magic Sea Horse Finds a Home __b__

Ocean Animals: The (Smallest) and the (Biggest) __a__

What's in a Fishpond? __c__

B. Choose one of the topics above. If you were going to write about it, which of these graphic organizers would you use to plan your writing? Circle it.   **Answers will vary.**

C. Circle the words that end in *est* under "Topics." Then write two sentences using those words.   **Sample Answers:**

1. The biggest animal in the ocean is the blue whale.

2. I think the smallest animal is krill.

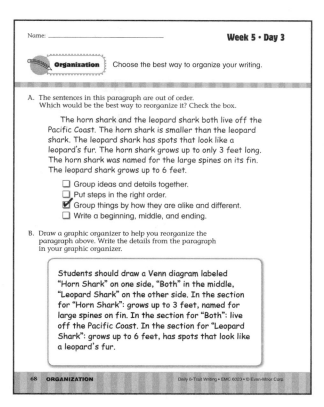

Name: _____   **Week 5 • Day 3**

Organization   Choose the best way to organize your writing.

A. The sentences in this paragraph are out of order. Which would be the best way to reorganize it? Check the box.

> The horn shark and the leopard shark both live off the Pacific Coast. The horn shark is smaller than the leopard shark. The leopard shark has spots that look like a leopard's fur. The horn shark grows up to only 3 feet long. The horn shark was named for the large spines on its fin. The leopard shark grows up to 6 feet.

☐ Group ideas and details together.
☐ Put steps in the right order.
☑ Group things by how they are alike and different.
☐ Write a beginning, middle, and ending.

B. Draw a graphic organizer to help you reorganize the paragraph above. Write the details from the paragraph in your graphic organizer.

> Students should draw a Venn diagram labeled "Horn Shark" on one side, "Both" in the middle, "Leopard Shark" on the other side. In the section for "Horn Shark": grows up to 3 feet, named for large spines on fin. In the section for "Both": live off the Pacific Coast. In the section for "Leopard Shark": grows up to 6 feet, has spots that look like a leopard's fur.

68 **ORGANIZATION**   Daily 6-Trait Writing • EMC 6023 • © Evan-Moor Corp.

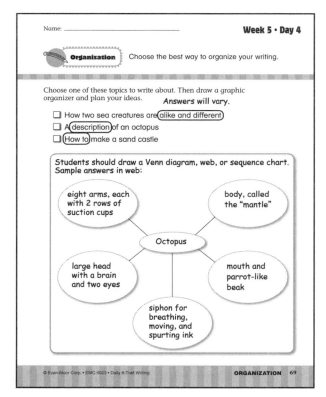

Name: _____   **Week 5 • Day 4**

Organization   Choose the best way to organize your writing.

Choose one of these topics to write about. Then draw a graphic organizer and plan your ideas.   **Answers will vary.**

☐ How two sea creatures are (alike and different)
☐ A (description) of an octopus
☐ (How to) make a sand castle

> Students should draw a Venn diagram, web, or sequence chart. Sample answers in web:
>
> eight arms, each with 2 rows of suction cups — Octopus
> body, called the "mantle"
> large head with a brain and two eyes
> mouth and parrot-like beak
> siphon for breathing, moving, and spurting ink

© Evan-Moor Corp. • EMC 6023 • Daily 6-Trait Writing   **ORGANIZATION** 69

DAY 3

Review the rule. Guide students through the activities.

- **Activity A:** Read the paragraph aloud. Then ask: *Is it easy to follow the writing?* (no) *Let's decide how this paragraph should be organized.* Ask: *What is this paragraph doing?* (telling how a horn shark and a leopard shark are alike and different) *How should we organize the details?* (Group the details by how the sharks are alike and different.)

- **Activity B:** Ask: *Which organizer do we often use when we compare and contrast?* (Venn diagram) Have students draw and label the diagram. Model filling in the diagram with details. For example, say: *The first sentence tells us that both sharks live off the Pacific Coast, so I'll write "live off Pacific Coast" in the middle section.* Then have students complete the activity.

DAY 4

Review the rule. Then guide students through the activity.

- Read the topics and have students circle any words in each prompt that give clues to the best form of organization. ("alike and different," "description," "how to") Have students determine which form of organization they would use for each prompt and the graphic organizer best suited for it. (Venn, web, sequence chart)

- Have students choose a topic and then draw their graphic organizers. Circulate to help students brainstorm details to include in their graphic organizers. Provide reference materials on ocean animals for students to use as necessary.

DAY 5 *Writing Prompt*

- *Use the ideas in the graphic organizer you created on Day 4 to write a well-organized paragraph.*

- *Be sure to use adjectives that end in **er** or **est** correctly.*

 **Organization**   The way you organize your writing depends on what you are writing about.

A. Makayla is writing about how to set up a new fish tank. Read the two explanations. Write an *X* next to the one that is organized more clearly.

☐ When you set up a fish tank, put plants and gravel in it. Put the fish in. But you have to make sure the tank is clean. The water has to sit for three days before the fish can go in. Use a heater to make the water warmer. My older brother helped me set up my newest fish tank.

☐ It's easy to set up a new fish tank. First, wash your new tank and put gravel in the bottom. Next, pour in water. Add plants, rocks, and caves. Then, put in a heater to warm up the water. Let the water sit for a few days. Finally, add your fish.

B. Write the four order words that were used in the second explanation.

_____ _____ _____ _____

C. Write the form of each of these adjectives that were used in the first explanation. Find and circle the words in the paragraph.

1. new, newer, _____

2. old, _____, oldest

3. _____, cleaner, cleanest

4. warm, _____, warmest

Organization Choose the best way to organize your writing to fit your topic and purpose.

A. Read the ways to organize different types of writing. Then read each topic. Write the letter of the best way to organize the topic.

> **Ways to Organize**
>
> a. **Compare and Contrast:** Group things by how they are alike and different.
> b. **Tell a Story:** Write a beginning, middle, and ending.
> c. **Describe:** Group ideas and details together.
> d. **Explain How:** Put steps in the right order.

Topics

How to Clean a Fish Tank _____

The Magic Sea Horse Finds a Home _____

Ocean Animals: The Smallest and the Biggest _____

What's in a Fishpond? _____

B. Choose one of the topics above. If you were going to write about it, which of these graphic organizers would you use to plan your writing? Circle it.

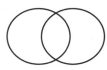 

C. Circle the words that end in *est* under "Topics." Then write two sentences using those words.

1. _____

2. _____

Organization   Choose the best way to organize your writing.

A. The sentences in this paragraph are out of order.
   Which would be the best way to reorganize it? Check the box.

> The horn shark and the leopard shark both live off the Pacific Coast. The horn shark is smaller than the leopard shark. The leopard shark has spots that look like a leopard's fur. The horn shark grows up to only 3 feet long. The horn shark was named for the large spines on its fin. The leopard shark grows up to 6 feet.

   ☐ Group ideas and details together.
   ☐ Put steps in the right order.
   ☐ Group things by how they are alike and different.
   ☐ Write a beginning, middle, and ending.

B. Draw a graphic organizer to help you reorganize the
   paragraph above. Write the details from the paragraph
   in your graphic organizer.

 **Organization** Choose the best way to organize your writing.

Choose one of these topics to write about. Then draw a graphic organizer and plan your ideas.

- ☐ How two sea creatures are alike and different
- ☐ A description of an octopus
- ☐ How to make a sand castle

WORD CHOICE
Choosing Strong Verbs and Adverbs

Refer to pages 6 and 7 to introduce or review the writing trait.

DAY 1

Read the rule aloud. Say: *Good writers choose their words carefully. They use strong, specific verbs instead of overused verbs, such as go and get.* Write the following sentence on the board: *The race car went around the track.* Underline **went** and point out that it is the past tense of **go**. Have students brainstorm stronger verbs to replace it. (e.g., *zoomed, zipped, flew*) Then guide students through the activities.

- **Activity A:** Read aloud the words in the box. Then read sentence 1 and ask: *Which verbs could you use instead of went to describe going slowly up a hill?* (**climbed, trudged, tramped**) Rewrite the sentence on the board with one of the stronger verbs. Repeat for the remaining sentences, pointing out that **got** is the past tense of **get**.

- **Activity B (Convention):** Write the words **to**, **too**, and **two** on the board. Say: *These words are **homophones**, or words that sound alike but have different meanings and spellings. Be sure to use the correct spellings when you write.*

DAY 2

Read the rule aloud. Point out that **vivid** means "clear and easy to picture." To demonstrate, read aloud the following sentences: *The baseball player **ran** around the bases. The baseball player **tore** around the bases.* Ask: *Which verb gives you a more vivid picture, **ran** or **tore**?* (**tore**) Then guide students through the activities.

- **Activity A:** Read aloud the first sentence of the paragraph and say: *The verbs **battled** and **played** both make sense, but **battled** tells me more. It tells me that the game was tough and exciting.* Have students complete the activity independently.

- **Activity B:** Have students name their favorite sports, and list them on the board. Then help students brainstorm verbs that go with each sport, using the verbs in the box for ideas. (e.g., football: **pass, punt, tackle**; basketball: **dribble, shoot, dunk**) Have students write their sentences. Then invite volunteers to read their sentences aloud.

- **Activity C (Convention):** Review the meanings of **to**, **too**, and **two** before students complete the activity on their own.

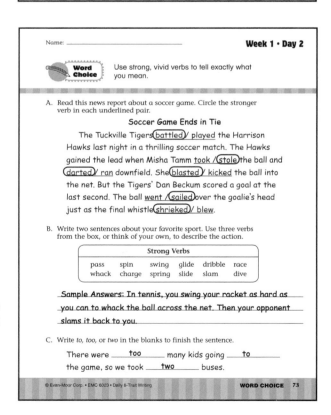

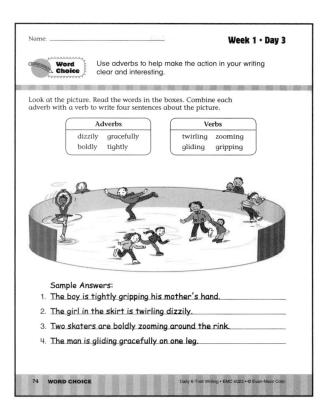

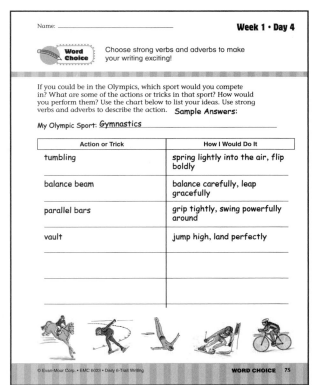

Read the rule aloud. Explain: *Adverbs are words that describe action, or **how** something is done. They often end in **ly**.* Write these sentences on the board: *The girl carefully stepped onto the ice. She skated smoothly across the rink.* Underline the verbs and circle the adverbs, pointing out that an adverb can come before or after a verb. Then guide students through the activity.

- Read aloud the adverbs and verbs. Then model choosing a word from each box to describe something in the picture. For example, say: *The boy and girl look like they're skating really fast, or **zooming**. They must be bold to go that fast. I'll write, "The kids are **zooming boldly** around the ice."*

- Have students write their sentences. Provide assistance as needed. Then invite volunteers to read their sentences aloud.

DAY 4

Read the rule aloud. Then guide students through the activity.

- Read the directions aloud. Together, brainstorm a variety of summer and winter Olympic sports. (swimming, track and field, gymnastics, skiing, snowboarding, figure skating, hockey, bobsled, tae kwon do, equestrian, volleyball, tennis, etc.)

- Model choosing a sport and using strong verbs and adverbs to describe it. For example, say: *I have always wanted to be an Olympic track star. I would compete in the **hurdles** event, **flying swiftly** around the track and **leaping confidently**. Then I would **dash quickly** across the finish line.*

- Have students choose a sport and complete their charts. Invite students who are writing about the same sport to work together.

DAY 5 *Writing Prompt*

- *Imagine that you have just competed in the Olympics! Write a paragraph telling what happened. Use the vivid verbs and adverbs you wrote in your chart on Day 4.*

- *Be sure to use **to**, **too**, and **two** correctly.*

Word Choice

Strong verbs make your writing come alive!
Avoid "tired" verbs, such as *go* and *get*.

A. Read each sentence. Look at the underlined verb. Write three
stronger verbs from the box that you could use instead.

Strong Verbs				
climbed	hopped	pranced	sprinted	trotted
dashed	jumped	raced	swooshed	trudged
galloped	leaped	skidded	tramped	tumbled

1. The hikers slowly <u>went</u> up to the top of the hill.

   _____   _____   _____

2. Tina and her horse <u>went</u> around the ring.

   _____   _____   _____

3. The two runners <u>got</u> across the finish line at the same time.

   _____   _____   _____

4. The gymnast <u>got</u> onto the balance beam too quickly and almost fell.

   _____   _____   _____

5. The skier <u>went</u> down the mountain.

   _____   _____   _____

B. Reread the sentences above. Find and circle the words *to, too,* and *two*.

 **Word Choice**

Use strong, vivid verbs to tell exactly what you mean.

A. Read this news report about a soccer game. Circle the stronger verb in each underlined pair.

Soccer Game Ends in Tie

The Tuckville Tigers <u>battled / played</u> the Harrison Hawks last night in a thrilling soccer match. The Hawks gained the lead when Misha Tamm <u>took / stole</u> the ball and <u>darted / ran</u> downfield. She <u>blasted / kicked</u> the ball into the net. But the Tigers' Dan Beckum scored a goal at the last second. The ball <u>went / sailed</u> over the goalie's head just as the final whistle <u>shrieked / blew</u>.

B. Write two sentences about your favorite sport. Use three verbs from the box, or think of your own, to describe the action.

Strong Verbs					
pass	spin	swing	glide	dribble	race
whack	charge	spring	slide	slam	dive

_____

_____

_____

C. Write *to, too,* or *two* in the blanks to finish the sentence.

There were _____ many kids going _____ the game, so we took _____ buses.

 **Word Choice**   Use adverbs to help make the action in your writing clear and interesting.

Look at the picture. Read the words in the boxes. Combine each adverb with a verb to write four sentences about the picture.

Adverbs
dizzily   gracefully
boldly   tightly

Verbs
twirling   zooming
gliding   gripping

1. _____

2. _____

3. _____

4. _____

Word Choice

Choose strong verbs and adverbs to make your writing exciting!

If you could be in the Olympics, which sport would you compete in? What are some of the actions or tricks in that sport? How would you perform them? Use the chart below to list your ideas. Use strong verbs and adverbs to describe the action.

My Olympic Sport: _____

Action or Trick	How I Would Do It

DAY 1

Read the rule aloud. Remind students that adjectives are words that describe nouns. They tell what kind (**scary** moth), how many (**six** legs), how much (**many** ants), and which one (**blue** butterfly). Then guide students through the activities.

- **Activity A:** Read the adjectives in the box. Say: *These are strong, colorful adjectives. They tell us more than "tired" adjectives such as* **big, gross,** *or* **pretty.** Direct students to look at the pictures and labels. Help them select two appropriate adjectives for each picture. For example, ask: *Which word could describe how a worm looks?* (**wiggly**) *What's another word in the box that tells about the worm?* (**moist**)

- **Activity B (Convention):** Write this sentence on the board: *The fat, round beetle scurried away.* Point out the comma and say: *Sometimes, you need a comma between two adjectives. A comma helps us see that these are two separate words that tell about the beetle.* Then have students complete the activity.

DAY 2

Read the rule aloud. Say: *Sometimes, using just one adjective isn't enough to fully describe something. Yesterday, we used pairs of adjectives to describe insects. Today, we'll look at more ways to combine adjectives.* Then guide students through the activities.

- **Activity A:** Read the letter aloud. Explain that amber is a hard, clear, yellowish-brown piece of fossilized tree sap. It sometimes contains an insect that was trapped in the sap before it hardened and fossilized.

  Ask: *What kind of word is each bold word in the letter?* (noun) Direct students to the word **present.** Ask: *What are the two words that describe* **present***?* (**special, unique**) Say: *Those adjectives tell us more about the necklace. Not only is it special to Jasmine, but it is also one of a kind, or unique.* Ask: *What is missing between the adjectives?* (a comma) Have students insert the comma and complete the activity.

- **Activity B:** Have students think of a special present they have received. Then have them write the sentence. Make sure they use a comma between the two adjectives.

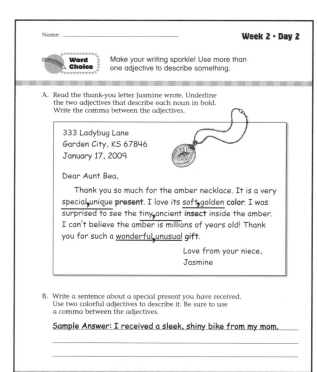

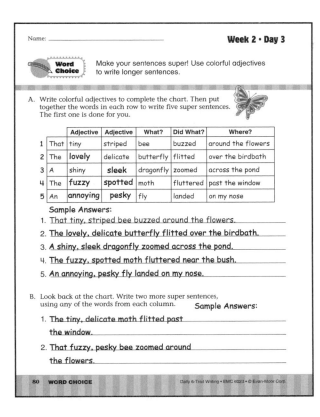

Name: _____   Week 2 • Day 3

Word Choice Make your sentences super! Use colorful adjectives to write longer sentences.

A. Write colorful adjectives to complete the chart. Then put together the words in each row to write five super sentences. The first one is done for you.

		Adjective	Adjective	What?	Did What?	Where?
1	That	tiny	striped	bee	buzzed	around the flowers
2	The	lovely	delicate	butterfly	flitted	over the birdbath
3	A	shiny	sleek	dragonfly	zoomed	across the pond
4	The	fuzzy	spotted	moth	fluttered	past the window
5	An	annoying	pesky	fly	landed	on my nose

Sample Answers:
1. That tiny, striped bee buzzed around the flowers.
2. The lovely, delicate butterfly flitted over the birdbath.
3. A shiny, sleek dragonfly zoomed across the pond.
4. The fuzzy, spotted moth fluttered near the bush.
5. An annoying, pesky fly landed on my nose.

B. Look back at the chart. Write two more super sentences, using any of the words from each column.   Sample Answers:

1. The tiny, delicate moth flitted past the window.

2. That fuzzy, pesky bee zoomed around the flowers.

80   WORD CHOICE   Daily 6-Trait Writing • EMC 6023 • © Evan-Moor Corp.

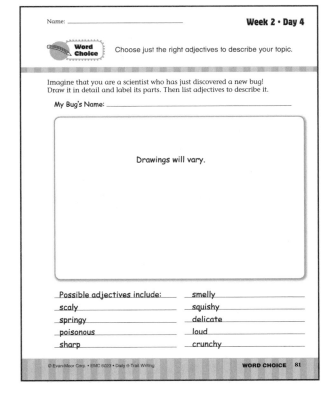

Name: _____   Week 2 • Day 4

Word Choice Choose just the right adjectives to describe your topic.

Imagine that you are a scientist who has just discovered a new bug! Draw it in detail and label its parts. Then list adjectives to describe it.

My Bug's Name: _____

Drawings will vary.

Possible adjectives include:	smelly
scaly	squishy
springy	delicate
poisonous	loud
sharp	crunchy

© Evan-Moor Corp. • EMC 6023 • Daily 6-Trait Writing   WORD CHOICE   81

DAY 3

Read the rule aloud. Say: *Using colorful adjectives can make your sentences longer and more interesting.* Then guide students through the activities.

- **Activity A:** Read aloud the words in the chart. Point out that six adjectives are missing. Help students brainstorm additional adjectives that could describe a butterfly. (e.g., **yellow, unusual**) Repeat for the remaining insects, making sure the first adjective in row 5 begins with a vowel.

  After students have filled in their charts, read the example sentence aloud slowly. Have students point to the words in the chart as you read them. Then have students complete the activity.

  Convention: Remind students to place a comma between the two adjectives in each sentence.

- **Activity B:** Direct students back to the chart. Model choosing one word or phrase from each column to write a new sentence. For example: *The lovely, striped dragonfly flitted over the birdbath.* Then have students write their own sentences and read them aloud.

DAY 4

Read the rule aloud. Then guide students through the activity.

- Brainstorm features of bugs with students. (e.g., how they eat, if they fly or walk, number of legs and wings, color, size, etc.) Then have students draw their made-up bug. When they finish drawing, demonstrate on the board how to label the parts of the bug. (e.g., wings, legs, antennae)

- Have students list adjectives to describe their bugs in as much detail as possible. Remind students to use strong, colorful adjectives.

DAY 5 *Writing Prompt*

- *Imagine that you are a scientist who has just discovered a new bug! Write a letter to another scientist, describing your bug in detail. Use your drawing and adjectives from Day 4.*

- *Be sure to write commas between adjectives.*

 **Word Choice**

Make your writing sparkle! Use colorful adjectives to describe people, places, animals, and things.

A. Read the adjectives in the box. Write two that describe each insect.

Colorful Adjectives

wiggly   spiky   tiny   squishy   shiny

spotted   hungry   moist   creepy   fuzzy

worm

adjectives: _____

_____

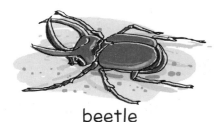
beetle

adjectives: _____

_____

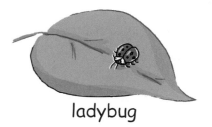
ladybug

adjectives: _____

_____

caterpillar

adjectives: _____

_____

B. Write a sentence about one of the bugs. Use two adjectives. Remember to use a comma between them.

_____

_____

Daily 6-Trait Writing • EMC 6023 • © Evan-Moor Corp.

Word Choice

Make your writing sparkle! Use more than one adjective to describe something.

A. Read the thank-you letter Jasmine wrote. Underline the two adjectives that describe each noun in bold. Write the comma between the adjectives.

333 Ladybug Lane
Garden City, KS 67846
January 17, 2009

Dear Aunt Bea,

   Thank you so much for the amber necklace. It is a very special unique **present**. I love its soft golden **color**. I was surprised to see the tiny ancient **insect** inside the amber. I can't believe the amber is millions of years old! Thank you for such a wonderful unusual **gift**.

                              Love from your niece,
                              Jasmine

B. Write a sentence about a special present you have received. Use two colorful adjectives to describe it. Be sure to use a comma between the adjectives.

_____

_____

_____

Name: _____

 **Word Choice**

Make your sentences super! Use colorful adjectives to write longer sentences.

A. Write colorful adjectives to complete the chart. Then put together the words in each row to write five super sentences. The first one is done for you.

		Adjective	Adjective	What?	Did What?	Where?
1	That	tiny	striped	bee	buzzed	around the flowers
2	The		delicate	butterfly	flitted	over the birdbath
3	A	shiny		dragonfly	zoomed	across the pond
4	The			moth	fluttered	past the window
5	An			fly	landed	on my nose

1. <u>That tiny, striped bee buzzed around the flowers.</u>

2. _____

3. _____

4. _____

5. _____

B. Look back at the chart. Write two more super sentences, using any of the words from each column.

1. _____

_____

2. _____

_____

Word Choice

Choose just the right adjectives to describe your topic.

Imagine that you are a scientist who has just discovered a new bug!
Draw it in detail and label its parts. Then list adjectives to describe it.

My Bug's Name: _____

_____   _____

_____   _____

_____   _____

_____   _____

DAY 1

Read the rule aloud. Say: *Good writers use exact nouns to say just what they mean. What do you think* **exact** *means?* (correct, just right) Say: *Weak nouns don't give as clear a picture as exact nouns do. For example, the word* **boat** *doesn't give as clear a picture as* **pirate ship, submarine,** *or* **canoe.** Then guide students through the activities.

- **Activity A:** Read the poems aloud. Direct students to the first underlined word in each poem. Ask: *Which word is more exact? Which one paints a clearer picture for the reader?* (**sailboat,** because it's a particular kind of boat) Continue comparing the weak and exact nouns. Then have students read and answer the questions.

- **Activity B (Convention):** Say: *A possessive noun tells who or what owns something. You add an apostrophe and s to a singular noun to make it possessive.* Then point out the word **brother's** in the poem and ask: *To whom does the old toy boat in the poem belong?* (brother) Model how to form a possessive by writing **brother's** on the board.

DAY 2

Read the rule aloud. Review: *Exact nouns help writers say exactly what they mean.* Read the following examples and have students picture the scene in their minds: *1) My grandma went on a boat last summer. 2) My grandma went on a cruise ship last summer.* Ask: *When I read sentence 2, how did the picture in your mind change?* (e.g., could see the type of boat, pictured it on the ocean filled with lots of people having fun) Then guide students through the activities.

- **Activity A:** Read the types of boats in the box aloud. Explain any types that students may be unfamiliar with, such as **oil tanker.** (a large ship used for transporting oil) Then read aloud the paragraphs and have students fill in the blanks. Ask a student to read the completed report aloud.

- **Activity B (Convention):** Direct students' attention to the first incomplete phrase. Then say: *Look at the word* **child** *under the first line. That tells us that the canoe belongs to the child. So what should we write on the line to finish the phrase?* (**child's**) Have students complete the activity.

Name: _____ **Week 3 • Day 1**

Word Choice — Use exact nouns in place of weak ones to make your writing stronger.

A. Read each poem. Look at the underlined words. Then answer the questions.

Poem A

Toy Boat

I found my brother's old toy boat,
And played with it today.
I added paper sails to it.
My <u>toy boat</u> flew—hooray!
A captain's <u>boat</u> it became,
And chugged around the bay.
A sailor's <u>boat</u> rescued me,
And carried me away.
An old man's <u>boat</u>, that was next.
I drifted in the sun.
The skipper's <u>boat</u> towed me in,
When my day was done.

Poem B

Toy Boat

I found my brother's old toy boat,
And played with it today.
I added paper sails to it.
My <u>sailboat</u> flew—hooray!
A captain's <u>ferry</u> it became,
And chugged around the bay.
A sailor's <u>lifeboat</u> rescued me,
And carried me away.
An old man's <u>rowboat</u>, that was next.
I drifted in the sun.
The skipper's <u>tugboat</u> towed me in,
When my day was done.

1. Which poem uses exact nouns? __Poem B__

2. Which exact nouns help the reader see what the speaker imagines while playing with the toy boat?

__sailboat, ferry, lifeboat, rowboat, tugboat__

B. Add an apostrophe and *s* to each word to make a possessive noun.

brother_'s_   captain_'s_   sailor_'s_   man_'s_   skipper_'s_

Name: _____ **Week 3 • Day 2**

Word Choice — Use exact nouns instead of weak ones.

A. Read the report. Write an exact noun for *boat* to complete each sentence. Use the words in the box.

Exact Nouns		
canoes	oil tankers	steamships
cruise ships	sailing ships	submarines

Can you imagine living without boats? For hundreds of years, Native Americans made ___canoes___ in order to trade with faraway tribes. In 1492, Columbus and his crew traveled to America in _sailing ships_ _____. Hundreds of years later, _steamships_ chugged across the ocean, bringing people to America.

Today, thousands of ___oil tankers___ carry oil all over the world. Some people work under the ocean on _submarines_ _____. Others enjoy vacations on large _cruise ships_ _____. Boats have always helped us get from one place to another.

B. Show who or what owns these things. Use the word under each line to write a possessive noun. Be sure to use an apostrophe and *s*.

a ___child's___ canoe   the ___explorer's___ journey
    (child)   (explorer)

a ___boat's___ oars   the ___ship's___ crew
    (boat)   (ship)

© Evan-Moor Corp. • EMC 6023 • Daily 6-Trait Writing   **WORD CHOICE** 85

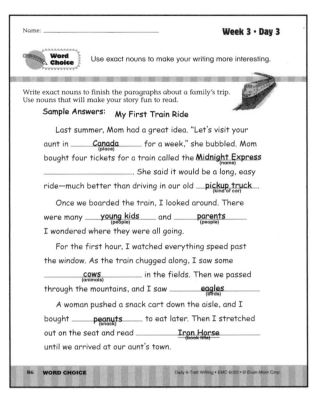

Name: _____   **Week 3 · Day 3**

Word Choice   Use exact nouns to make your writing more interesting.

Write exact nouns to finish the paragraphs about a family's trip. Use nouns that will make your story fun to read.

Sample Answers: My First Train Ride

Last summer, Mom had a great idea. "Let's visit your aunt in ____Canada____ for a week," she bubbled. Mom
(place)
bought four tickets for a train called the __Midnight Express__
(name)
_____. She said it would be a long, easy
ride—much better than driving in our old __pickup truck__.
(kind of car)

Once we boarded the train, I looked around. There were many ____young kids____ and ____parents____
(people)   (people)
I wondered where they were all going.

For the first hour, I watched everything speed past the window. As the train chugged along, I saw some
_____cows_____ in the fields. Then we passed
(animals)
through the mountains, and I saw ____eagles____
(birds)

A woman pushed a snack cart down the aisle, and I bought ____peanuts____ to eat later. Then I stretched
(snack)
out on the seat and read ____Iron Horse____
(book title)
until we arrived at our aunt's town.

86   **WORD CHOICE**   Daily 6-Trait Writing • EMC 6023 • © Evan-Moor Corp.

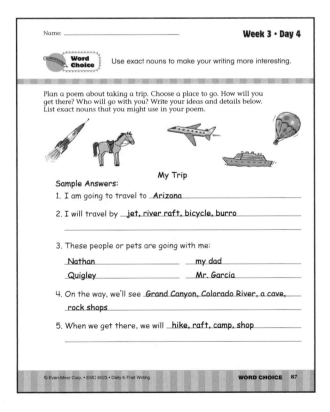

Name: _____   **Week 3 · Day 4**

Word Choice   Use exact nouns to make your writing more interesting.

Plan a poem about taking a trip. Choose a place to go. How will you get there? Who will go with you? Write your ideas and details below. List exact nouns that you might use in your poem.

My Trip

Sample Answers:

1. I am going to travel to _Arizona_

2. I will travel by _jet, river raft, bicycle, burro_

3. These people or pets are going with me:

   Nathan   _my dad_

   Quigley   _Mr. Garcia_

4. On the way, we'll see _Grand Canyon, Colorado River, a cave,_
   rock shops

5. When we get there, we will _hike, raft, camp, shop_

© Evan-Moor Corp. • EMC 6023 • Daily 6-Trait Writing   **WORD CHOICE**   87

DAY 3

Read the rule aloud. Say or write the following sentence and ask students to identify the weak noun: *I picked a flower.* (**flower**) Ask: *Can you name an exact noun that could be used instead of* **flower**? (e.g., daisy, rose, tulip) *When you use exact nouns, your writing becomes more clear and interesting.* Guide students through the activity.

- Read the first sentence of the first paragraph aloud and ask students to name exact nouns for a place that might fill in the blank. (e.g., Texas, New York City, Mexico) Read the rest of the paragraph, filling in the blanks with the general nouns underneath them.

- Have students complete the paragraph with exact nouns of their choice. Circulate to offer assistance. If a student uses general or weak nouns, push him or her to generate exact nouns. For example, ask: *What kind of horses did you see? What kind of candy bar did you buy?* Remind students to underline the book title. Then have students share their completed paragraphs to show the diversity of exact nouns.

DAY 4

Review the rule. Then guide students through the activity.

- Have students choose a place to write about. It can be somewhere they've been before, somewhere new, or somewhere imaginary.

- Brainstorm modes of transportation. Have students think about the various ways they would need to travel in order to reach their destination. Use the sample answers on the reduced page to the left to model filling in the questionnaire, if necessary. Then have students answer the questions. Circulate to prompt students to think of exact nouns.

DAY 5   *Writing Prompt*

- *Write a poem about taking a trip, using some of the exact nouns you listed on Day 4.*

- *Be sure to write singular possessive nouns with an apostrophe and* **s**.

 **Word Choice**

Use exact nouns in place of weak ones to make your writing stronger.

A. Read each poem. Look at the underlined words. Then answer the questions.

Poem A

Toy Boat

I found my brother's old toy boat,
And played with it today.
I added paper sails to it.
My <u>toy boat</u> flew—hooray!
A captain's <u>boat</u> it became,
And chugged around the bay.
A sailor's <u>boat</u> rescued me,
And carried me away.
An old man's <u>boat</u>, that was next.
I drifted in the sun.
The skipper's <u>boat</u> towed me in,
When my day was done.

Poem B

Toy Boat

I found my brother's old toy boat,
And played with it today.
I added paper sails to it.
My <u>sailboat</u> flew—hooray!
A captain's <u>ferry</u> it became,
And chugged around the bay.
A sailor's <u>lifeboat</u> rescued me,
And carried me away.
An old man's <u>rowboat</u>, that was next.
I drifted in the sun.
The skipper's <u>tugboat</u> towed me in,
When my day was done.

1. Which poem uses exact nouns? _____

2. Which exact nouns help the reader see what the speaker imagines while playing with the toy boat?

_____

B. Add an apostrophe and *s* to each word to make a possessive noun.

brother_____   captain_____   sailor_____   man_____   skipper_____

Word Choice   Use exact nouns instead of weak ones.

A. Read the report. Write an exact noun for *boat* to complete each sentence. Use the words in the box.

> **Exact Nouns**
>
> | | | |
> |---|---|---|
> | canoes | oil tankers | steamships |
> | cruise ships | sailing ships | submarines |

Can you imagine living without boats? For hundreds of years, Native Americans made _____ in order to trade with faraway tribes. In 1492, Columbus and his crew traveled to America in _____ _____. Hundreds of years later, _____ chugged across the ocean, bringing people to America.

Today, thousands of _____ carry oil all over the world. Some people work under the ocean on _____. Others enjoy vacations on large _____. Boats have always helped us get from one place to another.

B. Show who or what owns these things. Use the word under each line to write a possessive noun. Be sure to use an apostrophe and *s*.

a _____ canoe
(child)

the _____ journey
(explorer)

a _____ oars
(boat)

the _____ crew
(ship)

Word Choice   Use exact nouns to make your writing more interesting.

Write exact nouns to finish the paragraphs about a family's trip.
Use nouns that will make your story fun to read.

My First Train Ride

Last summer, Mom had a great idea. "Let's visit your

aunt in _____ for a week," she bubbled. Mom
             (place)

bought four tickets for a train called the _____
                                                 (name)

_____. She said it would be a long, easy

ride—much better than driving in our old _____.
                                              (kind of car)

Once we boarded the train, I looked around. There

were many _____ and _____.
               (people)   (people)

I wondered where they were all going.

For the first hour, I watched everything speed past

the window. As the train chugged along, I saw some

_____ in the fields. Then we passed
     (animals)

through the mountains, and I saw _____.
                                      (birds)

A woman pushed a snack cart down the aisle, and I

bought _____ to eat later. Then I stretched
          (snack)

out on the seat and read _____
                            (book title)

until we arrived at our aunt's town.

Word Choice

Use exact nouns to make your writing more interesting.

Plan a poem about taking a trip. Choose a place to go. How will you get there? Who will go with you? Write your ideas and details below. List exact nouns that you might use in your poem.

My Trip

1. I am going to travel to _____

2. I will travel by _____

   _____

3. These people or pets are going with me:

   _____   _____

   _____   _____

4. On the way, we'll see _____

   _____

5. When we get there, we will _____

   _____

WORD CHOICE
Using Similes and Metaphors

DAY 1

Read the rule aloud. Say: *A great way to describe something is by comparing it to something else.* Ask: *Which of these is more fun to read? 1) The boy's cheeks were red. or 2) The boy's cheeks were like ripe strawberries. (2) What does the sentence compare?* (red cheeks to strawberries) Because the comparison uses the word **like**, it's a simile. Then guide students through the activities.

- **Activity A:** Read the first simile aloud. Then ask: *What two things are being compared?* (snow and a feather) Have students complete the rest of the activity independently.

- **Activity B:** Read aloud the first simile. Ask: *Have you ever seen a cat's eyes? What bright objects might they remind you of?* (e.g., emeralds, diamonds, stars) Have students complete the activity and then share the similes they wrote.

- **Activity C (Convention):** Remind students that pronouns take the place of nouns. Then review the definition of a **possessive noun**. (a noun that shows belonging or ownership) Explain: *A possessive pronoun is one that takes the place of a possessive noun.* **His, her, its, my, our, your,** and **their** are all possessive pronouns.

DAY 2

Read the rule aloud. Then write this metaphor on the board: *The full moon was a pearl.* Say: *This metaphor compares the moon to a pearl because they are both round and pale white.* Then guide students through the activities.

- **Activity A:** Read the first metaphor. Ask: *What is being compared?* (music and a heartbeat) Have students fill in the word **heartbeat**. Then ask: *Why is music being compared to a heartbeat?* (Music has a beat, just like a heartbeat.) Have students complete the activity independently.

- **Activity B:** Help students brainstorm ideas by asking: *What things twinkle like stars?* (e.g., eyes, fireflies, diamonds, smiles) Have students complete the activity and share their metaphors.

Word Choice — Use similes to dress up your writing. A simile makes a comparison using the words *like* or *as.*

A. Circle the two things that are compared in each simile below.

1. The (snow) fell as quietly as a (feather).
2. The (girls) on the trampoline looked like (kangaroos).
3. The (rain) on the roof pounded like (drums) in a marching band.
4. The (hot chocolate) felt like a (volcano) erupting on my tongue.
5. The (train) sounded like a (thunderstorm) on its way through town.
6. The (kids) on the playground were as loud as (monkeys).

B. Finish the similes.   **Sample Answers:**

1. The kitten's eyes were as bright as __sparklers.__
2. The bird was as quick as __a dart.__
3. Spring is like __a warm hug from the sky.__

C. Read each sentence. Write the pronoun that replaces the underlined noun.

1. Brandon washed Brandon's hands.   __his__
2. Annie finished Annie's homework.   __her__
3. The students listened to the students' teacher.   __their__

Word Choice — Use metaphors to dress up your writing. A metaphor describes something by comparing it to something very different. It does not use *like* or *as.*

A. Read each metaphor. Then complete the sentence to tell what is being compared. Mark an X by the phrase that tells why the two words are being compared.

1. *The music is the heartbeat of the people.*
   Music is compared to a __heartbeat__ because they
   _____ are both loud.
   __X__ both have a beat.
   _____ are both necessary to stay alive.

2. *The candle became the sun, lighting the dark world.*
   A candle is compared to the __sun__ because they
   _____ are both in the sky.
   _____ both burn at night.
   __X__ both light the darkness.

3. *The children's voices were bells ringing through the streets.*
   The voices are compared to __bells__ because they
   __X__ sound musical.
   _____ are silent.
   _____ make the same sound over and over.

B. What could you compare to twinkling stars? Write a sentence containing a metaphor that compares something to stars.

__Sample Answer: Those lightning bugs were twinkling stars.__

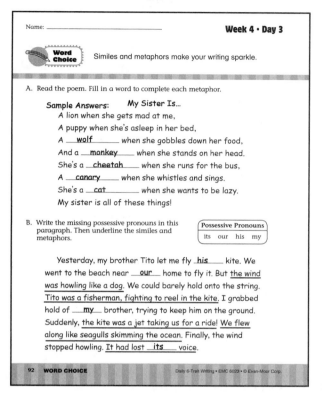

Read the rule aloud. Review: *Similes and metaphors compare two unlike things. A simile uses **like** or **as**. A metaphor says something **is** something else.* Then guide students through the activities.

- **Activity A:** Say: *Many similes and metaphors compare people to animals.* Ask: *Have you ever heard a person who is silly described as a monkey? Think about what qualities, or characteristics, we associate with animals. For example, what kind of person might be called an ox?* (someone who is strong) Read the poem together and have students select the best animal to complete each metaphor. Ask volunteers to read aloud their completed poems.

- **Activity B (Convention):** Review the list of possessive pronouns from Day 1. Then have students complete the activity. Afterward, read the paragraph aloud and have students check their pronouns. Finally, invite volunteers to identify the similes and metaphors they underlined.

DAY 4

Read the rule aloud. Then guide students through the activity.

- Have students think of a person they would like to write a poem about. Then brainstorm with students different qualities or characteristics those people could have. (e.g., kind, athletic, loyal, hardworking, tall) Have students list the qualities in the first column of the chart.

- Guide students in writing a metaphor or simile for each quality. Prompt by asking: *What could you compare the quality to? An animal? A sound or smell?* Point out the examples at the top of the chart. Then have students complete the activity. Circulate to provide assistance as necessary.

DAY 5 *Writing Prompt*

- *Write a poem with metaphors or similes to describe yourself or someone you know. Use the chart you completed on Day 4 to help you.*

- *Be sure to use possessive pronouns correctly.*

Word Choice

Use similes to dress up your writing. A simile makes a comparison using the words *like* or *as.*

A. Circle the two things that are compared in each simile below.

1. The snow fell as quietly as a feather.

2. The girls on the trampoline looked like kangaroos.

3. The rain on the roof pounded like drums in a marching band.

4. The hot chocolate felt like a volcano erupting on my tongue.

5. The train sounded like a thunderstorm on its way through town.

6. The kids on the playground were as loud as monkeys.

B. Finish the similes.

1. The kitten's eyes were as bright as _____.

2. The bird was as quick as _____.

3. Spring is like _____.

C. Read each sentence. Write the pronoun that replaces the underlined noun.

1. Brandon washed <u>Brandon's</u> hands.   _____

2. Annie finished <u>Annie's</u> homework.   _____

3. The students listened to <u>the students'</u> teacher.   _____

Word Choice

Use metaphors to dress up your writing. A metaphor describes something by comparing it to something very different. It does not use *like* or *as.*

A. Read each metaphor. Then complete the sentence to tell what is being compared. Mark an *X* by the phrase that tells why the two words are being compared.

1. *The music is the heartbeat of the people.*

    Music is compared to a _____ because they

    _____ are both loud.

    _____ both have a beat.

    _____ are both necessary to stay alive.

2. *The candle became the sun, lighting the dark world.*

    A candle is compared to the _____ because they

    _____ are both in the sky.

    _____ both burn at night.

    _____ both light the darkness.

3. *The children's voices were bells ringing through the streets.*

    The voices are compared to _____ because they

    _____ sound musical.

    _____ are silent.

    _____ make the same sound over and over.

B. What could you compare to twinkling stars? Write a sentence containing a metaphor that compares something to stars.

    _____

 **Word Choice**   Similes and metaphors make your writing sparkle.

A. Read the poem. Fill in a word to complete each metaphor.

My Sister Is...

A lion when she gets mad at me,

A puppy when she's asleep in her bed,

A _____ when she gobbles down her food,

And a _____ when she stands on her head.

She's a _____ when she runs for the bus,

A _____ when she whistles and sings.

She's a _____ when she wants to be lazy.

My sister is all of these things!

B. Write the missing possessive pronouns in this paragraph. Then underline the similes and metaphors.

Possessive Pronouns			
its	our	his	my

Yesterday, my brother Tito let me fly _____ kite. We

went to the beach near _____ home to fly it. But the wind

was howling like a dog. We could barely hold onto the string.

Tito was a fisherman, fighting to reel in the kite. I grabbed

hold of _____ brother, trying to keep him on the ground.

Suddenly, the kite was a jet taking us for a ride! We flew

along like seagulls skimming the ocean. Finally, the wind

stopped howling. It had lost _____ voice.

When you write a poem, use similes and metaphors to communicate your ideas.

Plan a poem that describes yourself, a friend, or a member of your family. List their qualities. Write similes or metaphors to describe the qualities.

Person: _____

Quality	Simile or Metaphor
Examples:	
funny	as funny as a pig on rollerskates
smart	like Albert Einstein
1. _____	_____
2. _____	_____
3. _____	_____
4. _____	_____
5. _____	_____
6. _____	_____

DAY 1

Read the rule aloud. Say: *Strong verbs grab your reader's attention because they make your writing more exciting!* Write the following and have students identify the verbs: *1) Lulu the pig trotted out to the road and plopped down. 2) Lulu the pig went out to the road and sat down.* Ask: *Which sentence sounds more interesting and exciting?* (the first) Then guide students through the activities.

- **Activity A:** Begin reading the article, pausing when you reach the first pair of verbs. Ask: *Which verb grabs your attention?* (**discovered**) *Why is it a stronger verb? What more does it tell us?* (Toby didn't just <u>see</u> his owner choking. He <u>came across</u> her suddenly.) Repeat for the rest of the article.

- **Activity B (Convention):** Point out the date in the first sentence of the news article. Say: *When a date appears in the middle of a sentence, use commas before and after the year.* Model the exercise on the board with your birthdate. Point out the commas.

DAY 2

Read the rule aloud. Ask: *Why do writers use colorful adjectives and strong adverbs?* (e.g., to make their writing interesting and to give more description) Then guide students through the activities.

- **Activity A (Convention):** Read the first sentence aloud and have students locate the date. Ask: *Where should there be commas?* (after **16** and **1996**) Then read aloud the article. Say: *Readers need details to understand our ideas. Without adjectives and adverbs, we are missing important details of the story.* Read the words in the box. Then guide students to fill in the blanks.

  Have a student read the completed article. Say: *Now the article is more interesting because we know more about what happened.* (e.g., how scary it was, how gentle Binti Jua was)

- **Activity B:** Brainstorm adjectives and adverbs with students. For example, ask: *What colorful adjectives could you use to describe Binti Jua?* (e.g., **brave, intelligent**) *What strong adverbs could you use to describe her actions?* (e.g., **cleverly, easily**) Have volunteers read their sentences.

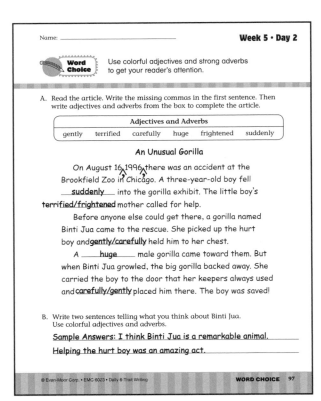

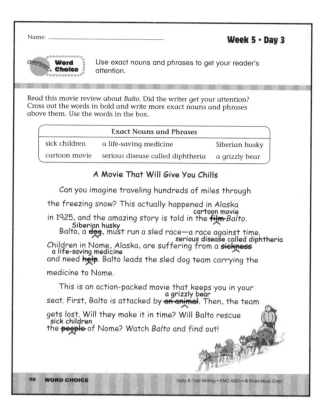

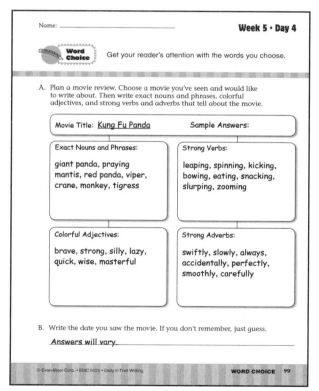

DAY 3

Read the rule aloud. Say: *Using exact nouns and phrases gets your reader's attention because exact words make your writing clear and easy to read.* Then guide students through the activity.

- Say: *A movie review tells what a movie is about. It also gives the opinion of the reviewer—what he or she liked and didn't like.* Then have students read the review. Ask: *Did the writer use many exact words and phrases?* (no)

- Read the exact phrases in the box. Then guide students to replace the words in bold in the review. For example, point out the word **film**. Ask: *Could the word **film** be more specific?* (yes) *Which exact phrase could take the place of **film**?* (**cartoon movie**) Continue with the remaining bold words. Read the revised review aloud. Ask: *Which review got and held your attention more, the original or the revision?*

DAY 4

Read the rule aloud. Then guide students through the activities.

- **Activity A:** Brainstorm movies that students have seen recently. Have students choose one movie they would like to write about. Then have them brainstorm exact nouns and phrases, colorful adjectives, strong verbs, and strong adverbs that describe the movie to fill in the graphic organizer.

- **Activity B (Convention):** Have students try to remember the date they saw the movie. If they can't remember, allow them to guess or use today's date. Use a student's answer to review proper comma placement.

DAY 5 *Writing Prompt*

- *Write a movie review. Use exact nouns and phrases, colorful adjectives, strong verbs, and strong adverbs from your Day 4 chart.*

- *In one sentence, include the date that you saw the movie. Be sure to write commas in the proper places.*

 **Word Choice**   Use strong verbs to get your reader's attention.

A. Read the news article. Look at the pairs of verbs under the lines. Write the one in each pair that is more attention-getting.

Dog Saves Owner

On March 23, 2007, something amazing happened in

Calvert, Maryland. Toby, a two-year-old golden retriever,

_____ his owner _____ to
(saw / discovered)   (trying / struggling)

breathe. Debbie Parkhurst had a piece of apple lodged in

her throat, and she was choking. Toby _____
(pushed / knocked)

her to the ground. Then he _____ on her
(jumped / got)

chest until he _____ the apple to
(forced / got)

_____ out. Toby _____ his
(come / pop)   (rescued / helped)

owner! For his efforts, Toby _____ the Dog
(received / got)

of the Year award.

B. When were you born? Write the date to finish the sentence.
Then write the date of a classmate's birthday. Be sure to write
the commas in the proper places.

On _____ I was born.

On _____ was born.

Word Choice

Use colorful adjectives and strong adverbs
to get your reader's attention.

A. Read the article. Write the missing commas in the first sentence. Then
   write adjectives and adverbs from the box to complete the article.

Adjectives and Adverbs
gently   terrified   carefully   huge   frightened   suddenly

An Unusual Gorilla

On August 16 1996 there was an accident at the
Brookfield Zoo in Chicago. A three-year-old boy fell
_____ into the gorilla exhibit. The little boy's
_____ mother called for help.

Before anyone else could get there, a gorilla named
Binti Jua came to the rescue. She picked up the hurt
boy and _____ held him to her chest.

A _____ male gorilla came toward them. But
when Binti Jua growled, the big gorilla backed away. She
carried the boy to the door that her keepers always used
and _____ placed him there. The boy was saved!

B. Write two sentences telling what you think about Binti Jua.
   Use colorful adjectives and adverbs.

_____

_____

 **Word Choice**

Use exact nouns and phrases to get your reader's attention.

Read this movie review about *Balto*. Did the writer get your attention? Cross out the words in bold and write more exact nouns and phrases above them. Use the words in the box.

Exact Nouns and Phrases		
sick children	a life-saving medicine	Siberian husky
cartoon movie	serious disease called diphtheria	a grizzly bear

A Movie That Will Give You Chills

Can you imagine traveling hundreds of miles through the freezing snow? This actually happened in Alaska in 1925, and the amazing story is told in the **film** *Balto*.

Balto, a **dog**, must run a sled race—a race against time. Children in Nome, Alaska, are suffering from a **sickness** and need **help**. Balto leads the sled dog team carrying the medicine to Nome.

This is an action-packed movie that keeps you in your seat. First, Balto is attacked by **an animal**. Then, the team gets lost. Will they make it in time? Will Balto rescue the **people** of Nome? Watch *Balto* and find out!

 **Word Choice**

Get your reader's attention with the words you choose.

A. Plan a movie review. Choose a movie you've seen and would like to write about. Then write exact nouns and phrases, colorful adjectives, and strong verbs and adverbs that tell about the movie.

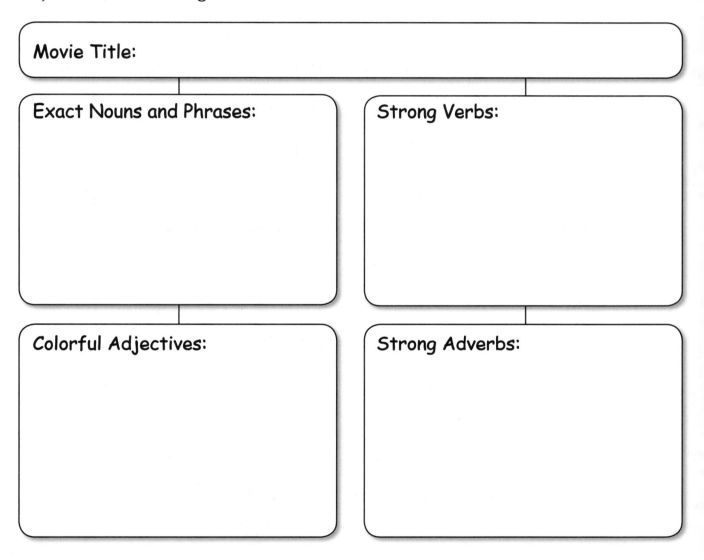

Movie Title:

Exact Nouns and Phrases:

Strong Verbs:

Colorful Adjectives:

Strong Adverbs:

B. Write the date you saw the movie. If you don't remember, just guess.

_____

SENTENCE FLUENCY
Varying Your Sentences

Refer to pages 6 and 7 to introduce or review the writing trait.

DAY 1

Read the rule aloud. Say: *Varying the way you write your sentences makes your writing sound more interesting. One way to do this is by starting each sentence differently.* Then guide students through the activities.

- **Activity A:** Have students read both reports and circle the sentence beginnings. Ask: *Which words did Rina start too many of her sentences with?* (**It, Its**) *Starting every sentence in the same way sounds boring. Vince began his sentences with both transition words* (**Then, Now, Instead**) *and pronouns* (**It, They**). *They make his report flow better.*

- **Activity B:** Reread the last sentence of Rina's report. Ask: *How could we revise this sentence so it begins differently?* Model writing it in different ways. (e.g., "The planet's farthest moon..."; "The farthest moon from Saturn...") Have students choose another sentence to rewrite on their own.

- **Activity C (Convention):** Write the words **have, has,** and **was** on the board. Say: *These are helping verbs. They come before certain verbs that need help.* Then point out the words **seen** and **saw** in Rina's report. Say: *These words are both past tense forms of the word **see**, but **seen** needs **have, has,** or **was** before it.* Have students complete the activity.

DAY 2

Read the rule aloud. Then guide students through the activities.

- **Activity A:** Direct students to the first pair of sentences. Say: *We need to choose which of these sounds best in the paragraph.* Read the first five lines of the paragraph aloud, once with each sentence choice. Ask: *Which sentence sounds better?* (Answers will vary.) Say: *The shorter sentence might sound better because it would separate the two longer sentences. But the other sentence flows well, too. You can write whichever you think sounds better within the paragraph.* Have students write their preferred sentence. Repeat the process with the second pair of sentences.

- **Activity B (Convention):** Review the rule for using a helping verb with **seen**. Have students correct the usage of **seen** and **saw**.

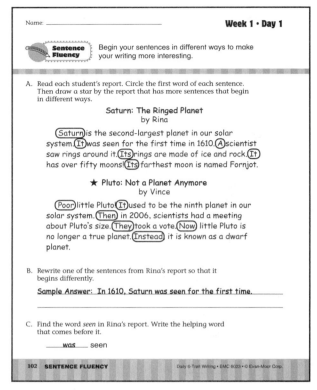

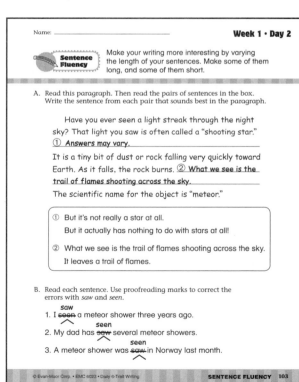

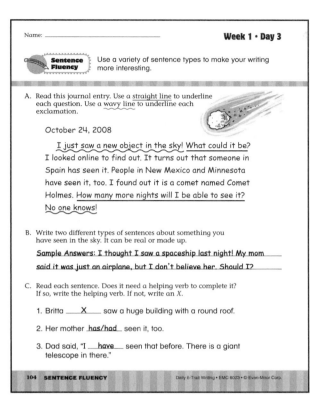

Read the rule aloud. Say: *Remember, there are four types of sentences: statements, questions, commands, and exclamations.* Review the meaning of each kind. Then guide students through the activities.

- **Activity A:** Remind students that a journal entry tells what you did on a certain day. Read aloud the entry and have students complete the underlining. Then ask: *How many kinds of sentences did the writer use?* (three)

- **Activity B:** Say: *Imagine that you are standing under the night sky. What could you see?* (stars, the moon, airplanes, etc.) *What would you tell about it? What kind of questions would you ask? What would make you write an exclamation?* Help students brainstorm ideas before completing the activity.

- **Activity C (Convention):** After students have completed the activity, go over the answers, reviewing the usage of **saw** and **seen**.

Read the rule aloud. Remind students that they can begin sentences in different ways, vary their lengths, and use different types of sentences to add variety to their writing. Guide students through the activity.

- Help students brainstorm what they might see in the night sky. (e.g., comet, UFO, new planet or star) Have students choose one to write about in their logs. Help them think of details by asking: *What did it look like? Did it move? Was there more than one? What did it remind you of?*

- Remind students that a logbook is like a scientist's journal, and that they don't have to use formal language or even complete sentences, but they do need to write the date.

Writing Prompt

- *Imagine that you are a scientist who saw something amazing in the night sky. Rewrite your notes from Day 4 as an article for a scientific magazine. Check that you have used a variety of sentence beginnings, sentence lengths, and sentence types.*

- *Be sure to use **saw** and **seen** correctly.*

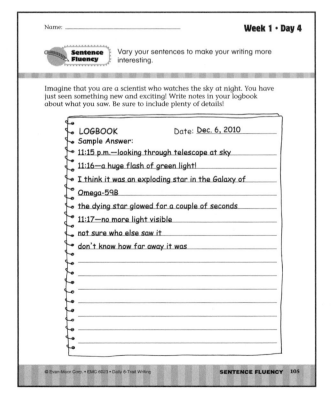

Sentence Fluency
Begin your sentences in different ways to make your writing more interesting.

A. Read each student's report. Circle the first word of each sentence. Then draw a star by the report that has more sentences that begin in different ways.

Saturn: The Ringed Planet
by Rina

Saturn is the second-largest planet in our solar system. It was seen for the first time in 1610. A scientist saw rings around it. Its rings are made of ice and rock. It has over fifty moons! Its farthest moon is named Fornjot.

Pluto: Not a Planet Anymore
by Vince

Poor little Pluto! It used to be the ninth planet in our solar system. Then, in 2006, scientists had a meeting about Pluto's size. They took a vote. Now, little Pluto is no longer a true planet. Instead, it is known as a dwarf planet.

B. Rewrite one of the sentences from Rina's report so that it begins differently.

_____

_____

C. Find the word *seen* in Rina's report. Write the helping word that comes before it.

_____ seen

 **Sentence Fluency**

Make your writing more interesting by varying the length of your sentences. Make some of them long, and some of them short.

A. Read this paragraph. Then read the pairs of sentences in the box. Write the sentence from each pair that sounds best in the paragraph.

Have you ever seen a light streak through the night sky? That light you saw is often called a "shooting star." ① _____

It is a tiny bit of dust or rock falling very quickly toward Earth. As it falls, the rock burns. ② _____

_____

The scientific name for the object is "meteor."

> ① But it's not really a star at all.
>
> But it actually has nothing to do with stars at all!
>
> ② What we see is the trail of flames shooting across the sky.
>
> It leaves a trail of flames.

B. Read each sentence. Use proofreading marks to correct the errors with *saw* and *seen*.

1. I seen a meteor shower three years ago.

2. My dad has saw several meteor showers.

3. A meteor shower was saw in Norway last month.

Sentence Fluency   Use a variety of sentence types to make your writing more interesting.

A. Read this journal entry. Use a <u>straight line</u> to underline each question. Use a <u>wavy line</u> to underline each exclamation.

October 24, 2008

   I just saw a new object in the sky! What could it be? I looked online to find out. It turns out that someone in Spain has seen it. People in New Mexico and Minnesota have seen it, too. I found out it is a comet named Comet Holmes. How many more nights will I be able to see it? No one knows!

B. Write two different types of sentences about something you have seen in the sky. It can be real or made up.

_____

_____

C. Read each sentence. Does it need a helping verb to complete it? If so, write the helping verb. If not, write an *X*.

1. Britta _____ saw a huge building with a round roof.

2. Her mother _____ seen it, too.

3. Dad said, "I _____ seen that before. There is a giant telescope in there."

Sentence Fluency   Vary your sentences to make your writing more interesting.

Imagine that you are a scientist who watches the sky at night. You have just seen something new and exciting! Write notes in your logbook about what you saw. Be sure to include plenty of details!

LOGBOOK   Date: _____

_____

_____

_____

_____

_____

_____

_____

_____

_____

_____

_____

_____

_____

_____

_____

_____

_____

DAY 1

Say: *We've learned that good writers use a variety of short and long sentences. Now, we'll learn how to combine short sentences into long sentences. Too many short sentences in a row can sound choppy.* Then read the rule aloud and guide students through the activities.

- **Activity A:** Read aloud both paragraphs, emphasizing the choppiness of the second. Ask: *Which paragraph sounds more choppy?* (the second) Say: *The first paragraph has both short and long sentences that flow smoothly from one to the next.*

- **Activity B (Convention):** Point out the compound sentences in the first paragraph of Activity A. Then say: *You can combine two short sentences into a compound sentence with a comma and a joining word such as **and, but,** or **or.*** Read aloud item 1 and model forming the new sentence on the board. Circle the comma and the joining word. Then have students copy the sentence and complete items 2 and 3.

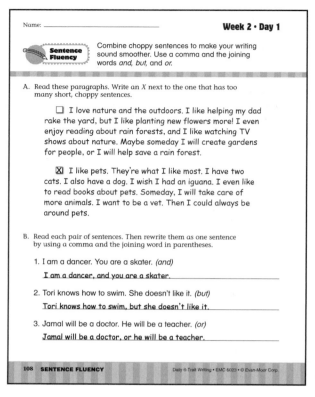

DAY 2

Read the rule aloud. Remind students that the **subject** of a sentence is the naming part. Write the following sentences on the board and have volunteers underline the subjects: <u>A cook</u> prepares food. <u>A server</u> brings you food. Then guide students through the activities.

- **Activity A:** Copy item 1 onto the board. Model combining the sentences. For example, say: *In the first sentence, the subject is "My mom," because that is who the sentence is about. In the second sentence, the subject is "My grandma." Both of them are nurses, so I can combine them into one subject: "My mom and grandma."* Write the new sentence on the board ("My mom and grandma are nurses"), noting the change from **is** to **are** to make it plural. Have students copy the sentence, and then have them attempt item 2 on their own.

- **Activity B:** Read aloud the paragraph and have students underline the sentences that can be combined. Check to be sure that students have underlined the correct sentences before having them complete the activity. Review the new sentences as a class.

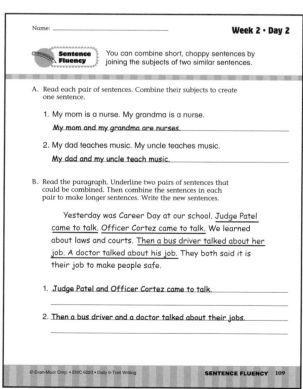

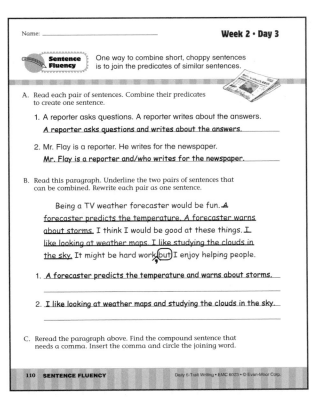

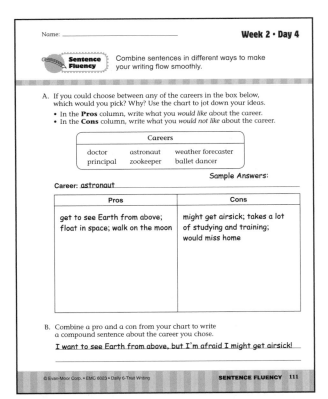

DAY 3

Read the rule aloud. Explain that the **predicate** of a sentence is the telling part—it tells about the subject or what the subject does. Write the following sentences on the board and have volunteers underline the predicates: *The teacher teaches her class. The principal leads the school.* Guide students through the activities.

- **Activity A:** Read aloud item 1. Then model writing the combined sentence as you say: *Both sentences have the same subject "A reporter," so we can join the predicates with the word **and**: "A reporter asks questions and writes about the answers."* Have students copy the sentence and complete item 2.

- **Activity B:** Read aloud the paragraph and have students identify the sentences to combine. Then have them write the new sentences.

- **Activity C (Convention):** If necessary, review the concept of compound sentences. Then have students complete the activity independently.

DAY 4

Read the rule aloud. Then guide students through the activities.

- **Activity A:** Read the career choices in the box aloud. Model choosing one and writing the pros and cons for it. For example, say: *I'd like to be a doctor. I enjoy helping people, so I'll write that in the **Pros** column. But I don't like the sight of blood, so I'll write that in the **Cons** column.* Help students brainstorm the pros and cons of each career. Then have students complete their charts.

- **Activity B (Convention):** Model using the chart to form a compound sentence. For example, write: *I like helping people, but I don't like blood.*

DAY 5 *Writing Prompt*

- *Use your chart from Day 4 to write a paragraph about a career you would like to have. Combine short sentences to make your writing flow.*

- *Be sure to use a comma and a joining word in compound sentences.*

Sentence Fluency

Combine choppy sentences to make your writing sound smoother. Use a comma and the joining words *and, but,* and *or.*

A. Read these paragraphs. Write an *X* next to the one that has too many short, choppy sentences.

☐ I love nature and the outdoors. I like helping my dad rake the yard, but I like planting new flowers more! I even enjoy reading about rain forests, and I like watching TV shows about nature. Maybe someday I will create gardens for people, or I will help save a rain forest.

☐ I like pets. They're what I like most. I have two cats. I also have a dog. I wish I had an iguana. I even like to read books about pets. Someday, I will take care of more animals. I want to be a vet. Then I could always be around pets.

B. Read each pair of sentences. Then rewrite them as one sentence by using a comma and the joining word in parentheses.

1. I am a dancer. You are a skater. *(and)*

_____

2. Tori knows how to swim. She doesn't like it. *(but)*

_____

3. Jamal will be a doctor. He will be a teacher. *(or)*

_____

 **Sentence Fluency** You can combine short, choppy sentences by joining the subjects of two similar sentences.

A. Read each pair of sentences. Combine their subjects to create one sentence.

1. My mom is a nurse. My grandma is a nurse.

_____

2. My dad teaches music. My uncle teaches music.

_____

B. Read the paragraph. Underline two pairs of sentences that could be combined. Then combine the sentences in each pair to make longer sentences. Write the new sentences.

Yesterday was Career Day at our school. Judge Patel came to talk. Officer Cortez came to talk. We learned about laws and courts. Then a bus driver talked about her job. A doctor talked about his job. They both said it is their job to make people safe.

1. _____

_____

2. _____

_____

Sentence Fluency

One way to combine short, choppy sentences is to join the predicates of similar sentences.

A. Read each pair of sentences. Combine their predicates to create one sentence.

1. A reporter asks questions. A reporter writes about the answers.

   _____

2. Mr. Flay is a reporter. He writes for the newspaper.

   _____

B. Read this paragraph. Underline the two pairs of sentences that can be combined. Rewrite each pair as one sentence.

> Being a TV weather forecaster would be fun. A forecaster predicts the temperature. A forecaster warns about storms. I think I would be good at these things. I like looking at weather maps. I like studying the clouds in the sky. It might be hard work but I enjoy helping people.

1. _____

   _____

2. _____

   _____

C. Reread the paragraph above. Find the compound sentence that needs a comma. Insert the comma and circle the joining word.

Sentence Fluency

Combine sentences in different ways to make your writing flow smoothly.

A. If you could choose between any of the careers in the box below, which would you pick? Why? Use the chart to jot down your ideas.

- In the **Pros** column, write what you *would like* about the career.
- In the **Cons** column, write what you *would not like* about the career.

Careers		
doctor	astronaut	weather forecaster
principal	zookeeper	ballet dancer

Career: _____

Pros	Cons

B. Combine a pro and a con from your chart to write a compound sentence about the career you chose.

_____

_____

SENTENCE FLUENCY
Revising Run-on and Rambling Sentences

DAY 1

Read the rule aloud. Say: *A run-on sentence is two sentences joined together without any punctuation, or with only a comma.* Review the types of end marks. Then guide students through the activities.

- **Activity A:** Have students read sentence 1 aloud. Ask: *Are there two complete sentences inside this sentence?* (yes) *What are they?* ("Have you seen my dollar" and "it is missing") Say: *This is a run-on sentence. Each of the complete sentences need a capital letter and an end mark.* Ask: *What should "Have you seen my dollar" end with?* (a question mark) *What should "it is missing" begin with?* (a capital I) Model using proofreading marks to insert punctuation and to indicate capitalization. Then have students complete the activity.

- **Activity B (Convention):** Read aloud the paragraph and have students raise their hands when they hear a run-on. Say: *Remember that a comma does not take the place of a period, a question mark, or an exclamation point. The comma needs to be replaced.* Model correcting the sentence. Then have students complete the activity.

DAY 2

Read the rule aloud. Say: *We've learned that combining short sentences into longer ones can make your writing smoother. But don't make your sentences too long. When you string together too many ideas with **and** and **but**, your writing rambles.* Guide students through the activities.

- **Activity A:** Read aloud the first paragraph, emphasizing each **and** and **but** and the lengthiness of each sentence. Then return to the second sentence. Say: *In this sentence, the writer has four different ideas. He talks about four different places. That's too many things in one sentence!* Have students complete the activity.

- **Activity B:** As a class, have students choose one of the rambling sentences to break into smaller sentences. Have them identify the different ideas within the sentence. Then have students write their revisions independently, and review them as a class. Point out that there is more than one way to break up each sentence.

Name: _____ **Week 3 • Day 1**

Sentence Fluency — A run-on sentence is two sentences joined together. Be sure to fix run-on sentences by breaking them up correctly.

A. Read each sentence. If it is a run-on sentence, use proofreading marks to insert the correct end mark and capitalize the first word in the second sentence.

1. Have you seen my dollar it is missing.

2. It is in your wallet.

3. I thought I dropped it here it is.

4. You should keep your wallet in a safe place.

5. Where will it be safe I always lose things!

B. Read the paragraph. Find the run-on sentences. Fix each one by deleting the comma and adding a period, a question mark, or an exclamation point.
Usage of periods vs. exclamation points may vary.

Have you ever bought anything at the Save Big Store? I got five dollars for my birthday I bought a few packs of baseball cards there. I also received a gift card I didn't know what to do with it. My dad said I could spend it at the Save Big Store, too! It is just like using cash. What did I do I went right back to the store. I bought more baseball cards!

Name: _____ **Week 3 • Day 2**

Sentence Fluency — Avoid long, rambling sentences with too many *ands* or *buts*. Fix a rambling sentence by breaking it into smaller sentences.

A. Read these paragraphs about coin collecting. Underline the rambling sentences. Circle the words *and* and *but* in each one.

Coin Collecting

Coin collecting is a great hobby because there are many different coins to collect from other countries. I have coins from Canada (and) I have a lot from the United States (but) I want more coins from Mexico, (and) I would like some coins from Europe.

Most coins show the name of the country they come from (and) they also show how much the coin is worth, (but) not all coins show the year they were made, (but) you can still collect those. I have coins that have pictures of people on them, (and) I also have coins that have pictures of animals or buildings (and) some coins don't have pictures on them at all.

B. Choose one of the rambling sentences from above. Rewrite it by breaking the sentence into smaller sentences.

Sample Answer: I have coins from Canada, and I have a lot from the U.S. I want more coins from Mexico, and I would like some coins from Europe.

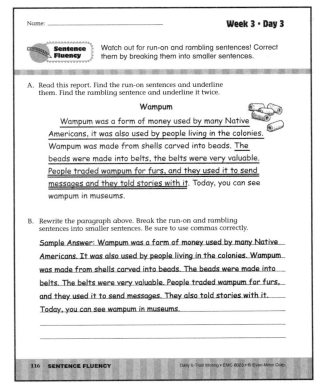

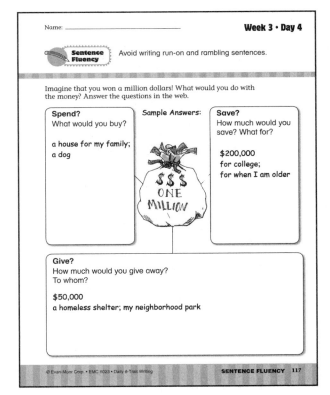

Read the rule aloud and review the difference between a run-on and a rambling sentence. Then guide students through the activities.

- **Activity A:** Read the paragraph aloud. Then have students underline the run-on and rambling sentences. Review the answers as a class, inviting students to explain why they underlined the sentences. (e.g., too many ideas; incorrectly punctuated)

- **Activity B:** Remind students that there can be more than one way to fix a run-on or rambling sentence. Then tell students to fix the sentences and rewrite the paragraph so it flows smoothly. Have them read their paragraphs aloud.

Convention: Have students proofread their paragraphs to make sure they have punctuated their sentences correctly. Say: *Remember that you cannot end a sentence, or keep it going, with only a comma.*

Read the rule aloud. Then guide students through the activity.

- Write the headings **Spend**, **Save**, and **Give** on the board. Then have students brainstorm a list of things they might do with a million dollars. Write students' suggestions under the correct headings.

- Have students fill in their individual webs. Circulate to assist as needed. Then invite students to share their responses.

Writing Prompt

- *Write a paragraph about what you would do if you won a million dollars! Use your ideas from Day 4. Be sure to avoid writing run-on and rambling sentences.*

- *Use commas and end punctuation correctly.*

Sentence Fluency

A run-on sentence is two sentences joined together. Be sure to fix run-on sentences by breaking them up correctly.

A. Read each sentence. If it is a run-on sentence, use proofreading marks to insert the correct end mark and capitalize the first word in the second sentence.

1. Have you seen my dollar it is missing.

2. It is in your wallet.

3. I thought I dropped it, here it is.

4. You should keep your wallet in a safe place.

5. Where will it be safe I always lose things!

B. Read the paragraph. Find the run-on sentences. Fix each one by deleting the comma and adding a period, a question mark, or an exclamation point.

   Have you ever bought anything at the Save Big Store? I got five dollars for my birthday, I bought a few packs of baseball cards there. I also received a gift card I didn't know what to do with it. My dad said I could spend it at the Save Big Store, too! It is just like using cash. What did I do, I went right back to the store. I bought more baseball cards!

Avoid long, rambling sentences with too many *ands* or *buts.* Fix a rambling sentence by breaking it into smaller sentences.

A. Read these paragraphs about coin collecting. Underline the rambling sentences. Circle the words *and* and *but* in each one.

Coin Collecting

Coin collecting is a great hobby because there are many different coins to collect from other countries. I have coins from Canada and I have a lot from the United States but I want more coins from Mexico, and I would like some coins from Europe.

Most coins show the name of the country they come from and they also show how much the coin is worth, but not all coins show the year they were made, but you can still collect those. I have coins that have pictures of people on them, and I also have coins that have pictures of animals or buildings and some coins don't have pictures on them at all.

B. Choose one of the rambling sentences from above. Rewrite it by breaking the sentence into smaller sentences.

_____

_____

_____

_____

Sentence Fluency

Watch out for run-on and rambling sentences! Correct them by breaking them into smaller sentences.

A. Read this report. Find the run-on sentences and underline them. Find the rambling sentence and underline it twice.

Wampum

Wampum was a form of money used by many Native Americans, it was also used by people living in the colonies. Wampum was made from shells carved into beads. The beads were made into belts, the belts were very valuable. People traded wampum for furs, and they used it to send messages and they told stories with it. Today, you can see wampum in museums.

B. Rewrite the paragraph above. Break the run-on and rambling sentences into smaller sentences. Be sure to use commas correctly.

_____

_____

_____

_____

_____

_____

_____

Sentence Fluency   Avoid writing run-on and rambling sentences.

Imagine that you won a million dollars! What would you do with the money? Answer the questions in the web.

Spend?
What would you buy?

Save?
How much would you save? What for?

$$$ ONE MILLION

Give?
How much would you give away?
To whom?

SENTENCE FLUENCY
More Ways to Combine Sentences

DAY 1

Say: *You already know how to combine sentences using* **and, but,** *and* **or.** *But there are a lot of other words you can use to join sentences.* Read the rule aloud. Then guide students through the activities.

- **Activity A:** Say: *The words* **so, because,** *and* **if** *relate, or connect, two ideas to each other.* Then read aloud sentence 1. Ask: *What is the joining word?* (**so**) *What two ideas or sentences does it join?* ("Roger decided..." and "he could play...") Have students complete sentences 2 and 3 independently. Review the answers as a class.

- **Activity B (Convention):** Say: *In Activity A, notice that each joining word is between the two shorter sentences.* Ask: *Is there a comma before the joining word?* (no) Say: *Unlike the words* **and, but,** *and* **or,** *these joining words usually don't need a comma when they are between two short sentences.*

  Read aloud item 1. Ask: *Which joining word makes the most sense between the two sentences?* (**because**) Say: *The second sentence gives a reason for the first, so* **because** *is the best word.* Then model forming the sentence on the board. Have students complete items 2 and 3 independently.

DAY 2

Review the joining words from Day 1. Then read the rule aloud. Guide students through the activities.

- **Activity A:** Say: *Sometimes a joining word is in the middle of a sentence. But it can also come at the beginning.* Read aloud sentence 1. Ask: *Which joining word begins this sentence?* (**When**) Say: *The writer used* **When** *because the sentence is about two things that happen at the same time.*

  Convention: Point out the comma in the middle of sentence 1. Say: *When you start a sentence with a joining word, you put a comma between the two joined sentences.* Then have students complete the activity. Review the answers as a class.

- **Activity B (Convention):** Model completing item 1, emphasizing the necessity of the comma. Then have students complete items 2 and 3.

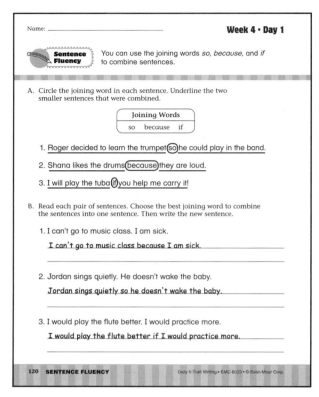

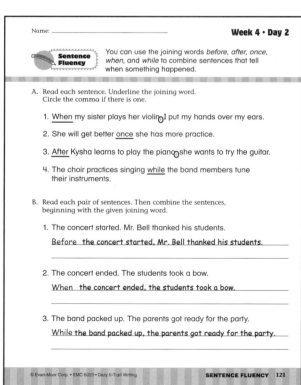

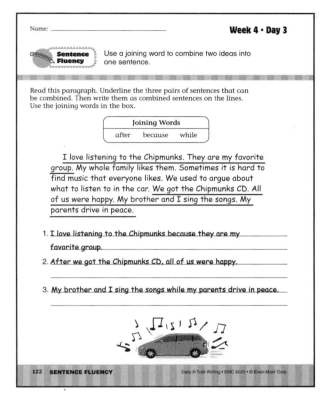

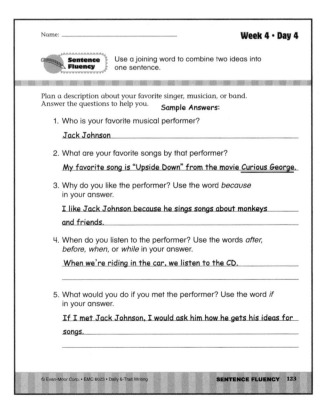

DAY 3

Read the rule aloud. Then guide students through the activity.

- Say: *Follow along as I read. Look for short sentences that relate to each other.* Then read aloud the paragraph. Ask: *Can the first sentence be joined with the second sentence?* (yes) Have students underline the sentences. Then have students find and underline the other two sentence pairs that can be combined.

- Model combining the first and second sentences. Ask: *Which joining word makes sense?* (**because**) *Should **because** be at the beginning of the sentence or in the middle?* Say: *The fact that the Chipmunks are the writer's favorite group explains why the writer loves listening to them. So, **because** should be in the middle. It does <u>not</u> need a comma before it.*

- **Convention:** Have students complete the activity independently. Remind students that if they begin a sentence with a joining word, they need to write a comma between the two ideas in the sentence. Review the rewritten sentences as a class.

DAY 4

Review the rule. Guide students through the activity.

- Help students brainstorm musical performers they like. Write their ideas on the board. Then have students choose a performer to write about.

- Go through questions 2–5 as a class, giving students time to write their answers. Then invite students to read their answers aloud and to explain whether they used a comma or not.

DAY 5 *Writing Prompt*

- *Use your answers from Day 4 to write a paragraph that describes your favorite singer, musician, or band. Try to use joining words such as **after, because, before, if, when,** or **while** in your sentences.*

- *If you begin a sentence with a joining word, write a comma between the two ideas in the sentence.*

Sentence Fluency You can use the joining words *so, because,* and *if* to combine sentences.

A. Circle the joining word in each sentence. Underline the two smaller sentences that were combined.

Joining Words
so   because   if

1. Roger decided to learn the trumpet so he could play in the band.

2. Shana likes the drums because they are loud.

3. I will play the tuba if you help me carry it!

B. Read each pair of sentences. Choose the best joining word to combine the sentences into one sentence. Then write the new sentence.

1. I can't go to music class. I am sick.

_____

_____

2. Jordan sings quietly. He doesn't wake the baby.

_____

_____

3. I would play the flute better. I would practice more.

_____

_____

Sentence Fluency

You can use the joining words *before, after, once, when,* and *while* to combine sentences that tell when something happened.

A. Read each sentence. Underline the joining word.
   Circle the comma if there is one.

   1. When my sister plays her violin, I put my hands over my ears.

   2. She will get better once she has more practice.

   3. After Kysha learns to play the piano, she wants to try the guitar.

   4. The choir practices singing while the band members tune their instruments.

B. Read each pair of sentences. Then combine the sentences, beginning with the given joining word.

   1. The concert started. Mr. Bell thanked his students.

      Before _____

      _____

   2. The concert ended. The students took a bow.

      When _____

      _____

   3. The band packed up. The parents got ready for the party.

      While _____

      _____

 **Sentence Fluency**   Use a joining word to combine two ideas into one sentence.

Read this paragraph. Underline the three pairs of sentences that can be combined. Then write them as combined sentences on the lines. Use the joining words in the box.

Joining Words
after   because   while

   I love listening to the Chipmunks. They are my favorite group. My whole family likes them. Sometimes it is hard to find music that everyone likes. We used to argue about what to listen to in the car. We got the Chipmunks CD. All of us were happy. My brother and I sing the songs. My parents drive in peace.

1. _____

_____

2. _____

_____

3. _____

_____

 **Sentence Fluency**   Use a joining word to combine two ideas into one sentence.

Plan a description about your favorite singer, musician, or band. Answer the questions to help you.

1. Who is your favorite musical performer?

_____

2. What are your favorite songs by that performer?

_____

3. Why do you like the performer? Use the word *because* in your answer.

_____

_____

4. When do you listen to the performer? Use the words *after, before, when,* or *while* in your answer.

_____

_____

5. What would you do if you met the performer? Use the word *if* in your answer.

_____

_____

SENTENCE FLUENCY
Writing a Smooth Paragraph

DAY 1

Read the rule aloud. Then say: *Now that we've learned how to make our sentences flow better, let's practice by writing smooth paragraphs. One way to make a paragraph smoother is to combine short, choppy sentences.* Review how to combine sentences with joining words such as **if, while, because, but, and**, and **or**. Then guide students through the activities.

- **Activity A:** Read the paragraph aloud, omitting the blanks. Then say: *This paragraph does not flow very well. The ideas need to be connected.* Then read the joining words in the box and have students write them in the correct places.

  Review the use of commas with joining words. Say: *When using **and, or,** or **but**, put a comma before the joining word. The other joining words don't need a comma when they're in the middle of a sentence. However, if you use one at the beginning of a sentence, write a comma between the two smaller sentences.* Have students complete the activity.

- **Activity B (Convention):** Say: *The past tense form of most verbs has **ed** on the end, such as **walked** or **baked**. But some past tense verbs don't end with **ed**. These are special.* Read aloud sentence 1. Ask: *Which verb should not have **ed** on the end?* (**speaked**) Say: *For the past tense, we say **spoke**.* Repeat the process for sentences 2 and 3.

DAY 2

Read the rule aloud. Then review: *A run-on sentence is two sentences joined together that should be separated by end punctuation. A rambling sentence has too many ideas and has words like **and** or **but** too many times.* Then guide students through the activities.

- **Activity A (Convention):** Read the paragraph aloud. Have students correct the verbs and underline the sentences that need fixing. Then review the answers as a class.

- **Activity B:** Remind students that there can be more than one way to fix a run-on or rambling sentence. Have students write their sentences, and invite volunteers to read what they wrote.

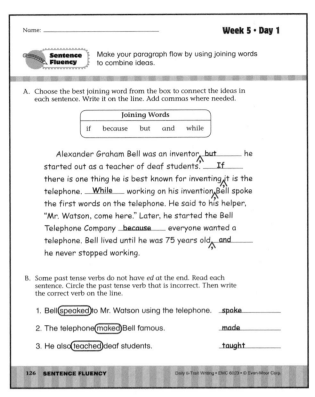

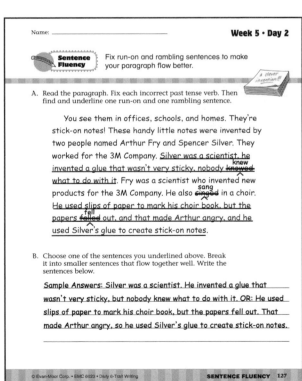

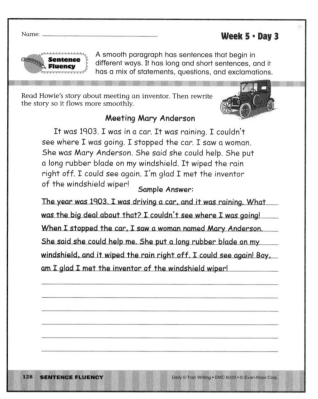

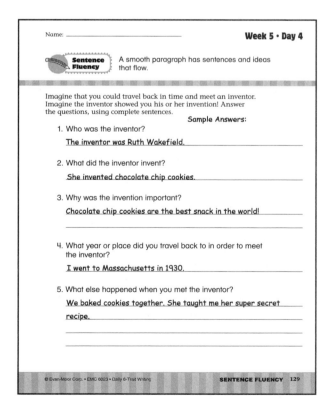

Read the rule aloud. Then guide students through the activity.

- Read the story aloud. Ask: *Which sentences begin the same way?* (the ones that begin with **It, I,** and **She**) Then ask: *Are any of the sentences questions or exclamations?* (no) *Are there both long and short sentences?* (no—mostly just short)

- Have students work independently or in pairs to rewrite the story. Circulate to provide assistance as necessary. Then invite students to read aloud their "smooth" revisions.

- **Convention:** Invite students to find the irregular past tense verbs in the story. (e.g., **was, saw, said, put, met**)

Read the rule aloud. Then guide students through the activity.

- Say: *Think of some of your favorite toys or gadgets. Have you ever wondered who invented them?* Brainstorm a list of simple inventions that students might enjoy researching. Use the Internet to find their inventors, and write the names on the board. Have students choose an inventor to write about.

- Guide students through the questions. For example, say: *Imagine what would happen if you met that inventor!* Model completing items 2–5 by using an inventor you know or using the sample answers on the reduced page to the left. Circulate to assist students as they complete the activity.

Writing Prompt

- *Use your answers from Day 4 to write a story about going back in time and meeting an inventor. Make your story flow smoothly from sentence to sentence.*

- *Be sure to use the correct past tense form of verbs.*

Sentence Fluency   Make your paragraph flow by using joining words to combine ideas.

A. Choose the best joining word from the box to connect the ideas in each sentence. Write it on the line. Add commas where needed.

Joining Words
if   because   but   and   while

Alexander Graham Bell was an inventor _____ he started out as a teacher of deaf students. _____ there is one thing he is best known for inventing it is the telephone. _____ working on his invention Bell spoke the first words on the telephone. He said to his helper, "Mr. Watson, come here." Later, he started the Bell Telephone Company _____ everyone wanted a telephone. Bell lived until he was 75 years old _____ he never stopped working.

B. Some past tense verbs do not have *ed* at the end. Read each sentence. Circle the past tense verb that is incorrect. Then write the correct verb on the line.

1. Bell speaked to Mr. Watson using the telephone. _____

2. The telephone maked Bell famous. _____

3. He also teached deaf students. _____

Sentence Fluency

Fix run-on and rambling sentences to make your paragraph flow better.

A clever invention!!!

A. Read the paragraph. Fix each incorrect past tense verb. Then find and underline one run-on and one rambling sentence.

You see them in offices, schools, and homes. They're stick-on notes! These handy little notes were invented by two people named Arthur Fry and Spencer Silver. They worked for the 3M Company. Silver was a scientist, he invented a glue that wasn't very sticky, nobody knowed what to do with it. Fry was a scientist who invented new products for the 3M Company. He also singed in a choir. He used slips of paper to mark his choir book, but the papers falled out, and that made Arthur angry, and he used Silver's glue to create stick-on notes.

B. Choose one of the sentences you underlined above. Break it into smaller sentences that flow together well. Write the sentences below.

_____

_____

_____

_____

_____

Sentence Fluency

A smooth paragraph has sentences that begin in different ways. It has long and short sentences, and it has a mix of statements, questions, and exclamations.

Read Howie's story about meeting an inventor. Then rewrite the story so it flows more smoothly.

Meeting Mary Anderson

It was 1903. I was in a car. It was raining. I couldn't see where I was going. I stopped the car. I saw a woman. She was Mary Anderson. She said she could help. She put a long rubber blade on my windshield. It wiped the rain right off. I could see again. I'm glad I met the inventor of the windshield wiper!

_____

_____

_____

_____

_____

_____

_____

_____

_____

_____

Sentence Fluency

A smooth paragraph has sentences and ideas that flow.

Imagine that you could travel back in time and meet an inventor. Imagine the inventor showed you his or her invention! Answer the questions, using complete sentences.

1. Who was the inventor?

   _____

2. What did the inventor invent?

   _____

3. Why was the invention important?

   _____

   _____

4. What year or place did you travel back to in order to meet the inventor?

   _____

5. What else happened when you met the inventor?

   _____

   _____

   _____

   _____

DAY 1

Read the rule aloud. Say: *Good writers make sure their writing has a distinct "voice," or style. You can make your voice sound playful, serious, or exciting to fit your purpose.* Then guide students through the activities.

- **Activity A:** Read the article aloud. Say: *This writer wanted to write about a discovery in a fun way, so the writer used a funny, playful voice.* Read aloud the question and list of responses. Ask: *What surprise does the reader find out?* (Egyptian kings played checkers.) *How is the title funny?* (It makes you imagine a mummy playing a game.) *What silly thought does the writer leave us with?* (asking a mummy to play checkers)

- **Activity B:** Read the first sentence together. Ask: *Does this sentence fit the style of the story?* (Yes, because it's a silly idea.) Have students complete the rest of the activity independently.

- **Activity C (Convention):** Remind students that a contraction is two words joined together to form a shorter word. An apostrophe takes the place of the letter or letters that have been left out. Say: *Many contractions are made from the word **is**.* Write **it is, that is,** and **what is** on the board and model turning them into **it's, that's,** and **what's.** Then have students complete the activity.

DAY 2

Read the rule aloud. Then guide students through the activities.

- **Activity A:** Read the story aloud. Say: *Austin wanted his reader to know how important this event was to him, so he wrote in a serious, formal voice.* Then help students find language that makes the story sound formal, such as using **father** instead of **dad**; **young child** instead of **little kid**; **receive** instead of **get**; and **inquired** instead of **asked**.

- **Activity B:** Brainstorm with students what they might write about. (e.g., a meaningful gift, a special time they had with a relative, etc.) After students write their sentences, ask volunteers to share what they wrote.

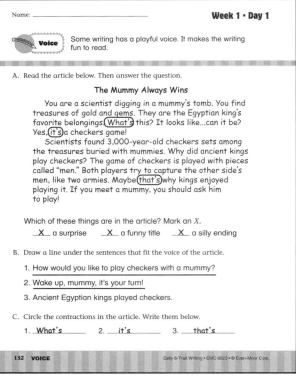

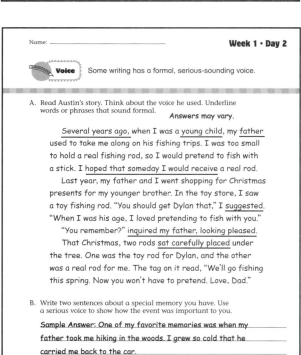

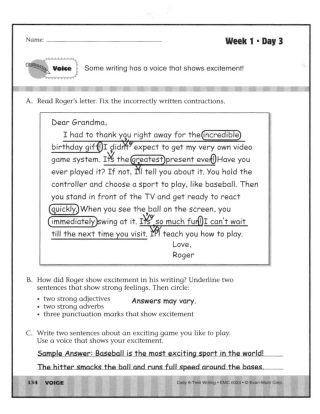

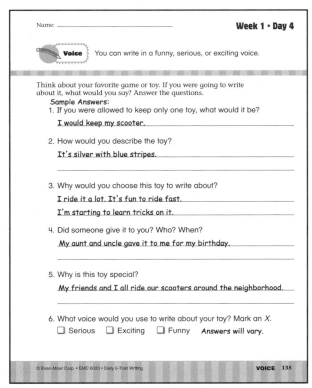

Read the rule aloud. Then guide students through the activities.

- **Activity A (Convention):** Read the letter aloud. Say: *Roger wanted his grandmother to know how excited he was about his new game system, so he wrote his letter in an exciting voice. But he wrote some contractions incorrectly.* Point out the word **didnt'**. Ask: *Where should the apostrophe be?* (between **n** and **t**) Have students find and correct the remaining contractions. Point out that when **its** is spelled without an apostrophe, it becomes a possessive pronoun, as in "its screen." So it is particularly important to remember the apostrophe when you are writing the contraction for "it is."

- **Activity B:** Say: *Let's find what Roger did to give his letter an exciting voice.* Guide students through the letter, helping them identify the modifiers, exclamation points, and sentences with feelings.

- **Activity C:** Brainstorm with students exciting games they like to play. (e.g., team sports, video games) Then have them write their sentences, making sure they use an exciting voice.

DAY 4

Read the rule aloud. Then guide students through the activity.

- Have students brainstorm their favorite or most important toys and games. Then have them answer questions 1–5 independently.

- For question 6, say: *Think about which voice would be best to tell about your toy. That might depend on your answers to the questions. For example, if it's a doll that was your grandmother's, you might want to use a serious voice. If it's a game that requires speed and skill, you might want to use an exciting voice.*

DAY 5 *Writing Prompt*

- *Use your answers to the questions on Day 4 to write about your favorite game or toy. Use a serious, exciting, or funny voice.*

- *Be sure to spell contractions correctly.*

 **Voice** Some writing has a playful voice. It makes the writing fun to read.

A. Read the article below. Then answer the question.

The Mummy Always Wins

You are a scientist digging in a mummy's tomb. You find treasures of gold and gems. They are the Egyptian king's favorite belongings. What's this? It looks like...can it be? Yes, it's a checkers game!

Scientists found 3,000-year-old checkers sets among the treasures buried with mummies. Why did ancient kings play checkers? The game of checkers is played with pieces called "men." Both players try to capture the other side's men, like two armies. Maybe that's why kings enjoyed playing it. If you meet a mummy, you should ask him to play!

Which of these things are in the article? Mark an *X*.

_____ a surprise   _____ a funny title   _____ a silly ending

B. Draw a line under the sentences that fit the voice of the article.

1. How would you like to play checkers with a mummy?

2. Wake up, mummy, it's your turn!

3. Ancient Egyptian kings played checkers.

C. Circle the contractions in the article. Write them below.

1. _____   2. _____   3. _____

 **Voice** Some writing has a formal, serious-sounding voice.

A. Read Austin's story. Think about the voice he used. Underline words or phrases that sound formal.

Several years ago, when I was a young child, my father used to take me along on his fishing trips. I was too small to hold a real fishing rod, so I would pretend to fish with a stick. I hoped that someday I would receive a real rod.

Last year, my father and I went shopping for Christmas presents for my younger brother. In the toy store, I saw a toy fishing rod. "You should get Dylan that," I suggested. "When I was his age, I loved pretending to fish with you."

"You remember?" inquired my father, looking pleased.

That Christmas, two rods sat carefully placed under the tree. One was the toy rod for Dylan, and the other was a real rod for me. The tag on it read, "We'll go fishing this spring. Now you won't have to pretend. Love, Dad."

B. Write two sentences about a special memory you have. Use a serious voice to show how the event was important to you.

_____

_____

_____

 **Voice** Some writing has a voice that shows excitement!

A. Read Roger's letter. Fix the incorrectly written contractions.

> Dear Grandma,
>
> I had to thank you right away for the incredible birthday gift! I didnt' expect to get my very own video game system. Its the greatest present ever! Have you ever played it? If not, Ill tell you about it. You hold the controller and choose a sport to play, like baseball. Then you stand in front of the TV and get ready to react quickly. When you see the ball on the screen, you immediately swing at it. Its' so much fun! I can't wait till the next time you visit. Il'l teach you how to play.
>
> Love,
> Roger

B. How did Roger show excitement in his writing? Underline two sentences that show strong feelings. Then circle:

  • two strong adjectives
  • two strong adverbs
  • three punctuation marks that show excitement

C. Write two sentences about an exciting game you like to play. Use a voice that shows your excitement.

_____

_____

 **Voice** You can write in a funny, serious, or exciting voice.

Think about your favorite game or toy. If you were going to write about it, what would you say? Answer the questions.

1. If you were allowed to keep only one toy, what would it be?

   _____

2. How would you describe the toy?

   _____

   _____

3. Why would you choose this toy to write about?

   _____

   _____

4. Did someone give it to you? Who? When?

   _____

   _____

5. Why is this toy special?

   _____

   _____

6. What voice would you use to write about your toy? Mark an *X*.
   ☐ Serious   ☐ Exciting   ☐ Funny

DAY 1

Read the rule aloud. Remind students that formal language is the proper, or standard, way to speak and write. Informal language is the way we speak with friends and family. Then say: *The kind of language we use depends on our **purpose** and **audience**. Your purpose is why you're writing. Your audience is who will read your writing.* Then guide students through the activities.

- **Activity A:** Read the e-mail and picture caption aloud. Point out that they are both written for the same purpose (to tell about a mask), but the audiences are different and, therefore, so are the styles of language. Have students identify the audience for the e-mail. (Uncle Ravi) Ask: *What kind of language did Chitra use?* (informal) Help students identify language and conventions that make the writing informal. (e.g., **Hi, Here's a pic of me, Fri., Wish you could**) Repeat for the picture caption, pointing out that the more formal-sounding language is intended for an audience whom the writer doesn't know personally.

- **Activity B (Convention):** Review that quotation marks are used to show the exact words someone says. Then have students complete the activity.

DAY 2

Read the rule aloud. Then guide students through the activities.

- **Activity A:** Read the report aloud. Ask: *Is this written in formal or informal language?* (formal) *How can you tell?* (no slang; **she is** instead of contraction; states facts clearly)

- **Activity B:** Read the sentences aloud. Have students choose the ones that use formal language. Then ask: *Why didn't you choose the other sentences?* (They sound too informal.) Have students write their paragraphs and share them.

- **Activity C (Convention):** Remind students: *Quotation marks go around the exact words of a speaker.* Brainstorm with students what Lila might say and how she would say it. Ask: *Would Lila use formal or informal language when speaking to a friend?* Then have students complete the activity.

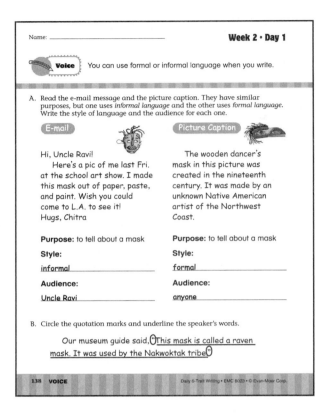

Name: _____   **Week 2 · Day 1**

Voice You can use formal or informal language when you write.

A. Read the e-mail message and the picture caption. They have similar purposes, but one uses *informal language* and the other uses *formal language*. Write the style of language and the audience for each one.

E-mail

Hi, Uncle Ravi!
  Here's a pic of me last Fri. at the school art show. I made this mask out of paper, paste, and paint. Wish you could come to L.A. to see it!
Hugs, Chitra

Purpose: to tell about a mask
Style:
informal
Audience:
Uncle Ravi

Picture Caption

  The wooden dancer's mask in this picture was created in the nineteenth century. It was made by an unknown Native American artist of the Northwest Coast.

Purpose: to tell about a mask
Style:
formal
Audience:
anyone

B. Circle the quotation marks and underline the speaker's words.

  Our museum guide said, "This mask is called a raven mask. It was used by the Nakwoktak tribe."

138 VOICE   Daily 6-Trait Writing • EMC 6023 • © Evan-Moor Corp.

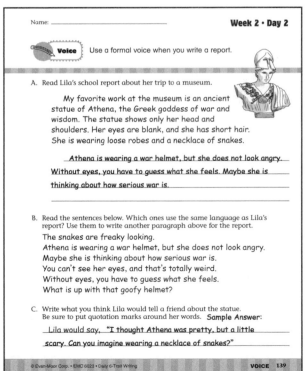

Name: _____   **Week 2 · Day 2**

Voice Use a formal voice when you write a report.

A. Read Lila's school report about her trip to a museum.

  My favorite work at the museum is an ancient statue of Athena, the Greek goddess of war and wisdom. The statue shows only her head and shoulders. Her eyes are blank, and she has short hair. She is wearing loose robes and a necklace of snakes.

  Athena is wearing a war helmet, but she does not look angry. Without eyes, you have to guess what she feels. Maybe she is thinking about how serious war is.

B. Read the sentences below. Which ones use the same language as Lila's report? Use them to write another paragraph above for the report.

The snakes are freaky looking.
Athena is wearing a war helmet, but she does not look angry.
Maybe she is thinking about how serious war is.
You can't see her eyes, and that's totally weird.
Without eyes, you have to guess what she feels.
What is up with that goofy helmet?

C. Write what you think Lila would tell a friend about the statue. Be sure to put quotation marks around her words. **Sample Answer:**

  Lila would say, "I thought Athena was pretty, but a little scary. Can you imagine wearing a necklace of snakes?"

© Evan-Moor Corp. • EMC 6023 • Daily 6-Trait Writing   **VOICE** 139

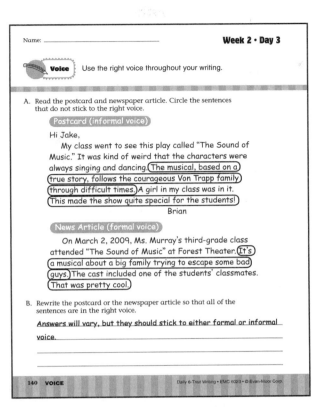

Voice Use the right voice throughout your writing.

A. Read the postcard and newspaper article. Circle the sentences that do not stick to the right voice.

Postcard (informal voice)

Hi Jake,
   My class went to see this play called "The Sound of Music." It was kind of weird that the characters were always singing and dancing. The musical, based on a true story, follows the courageous Von Trapp family through difficult times. A girl in my class was in it. This made the show quite special for the students!
                                                            Brian

News Article (formal voice)

   On March 2, 2009, Ms. Murray's third-grade class attended "The Sound of Music" at Forest Theater. It's a musical about a big family trying to escape some bad guys. The cast included one of the students' classmates. That was pretty cool.

B. Rewrite the postcard or the newspaper article so that all of the sentences are in the right voice.

Answers will vary, but they should stick to either formal or informal voice.

140   VOICE   Daily 6-Trait Writing • EMC 6023 • © Evan-Moor Corp.

Name:

Week 2 • Day 4

Voice Use formal or informal language in your writing.

Interview a partner about something interesting he or she has done or seen.

1. What did you do or see?
   went on a vacation, went skiing and snowshoeing

2. When did this happen?
   last winter

3. Where did it happen?
   Traverse City, Michigan

4. Whom did you go with or see?
   my family

5. Why was this so interesting or special? Write your partner's exact words.
   Jamie said, "It was a special trip because my family loves to ski together."

© Evan-Moor Corp. • EMC 6023 • Daily 6-Trait Writing   VOICE   141

DAY 3

Read the rule aloud. Say: *Always stick to the voice that is best for your form of writing and audience.* Then guide students through the activities.

- **Activity A:** Read aloud the postcard. Remind students that a postcard uses informal voice. Ask: *Do all of these sentences use an informal voice?* (no) Have students identify which sentences sound more formal. (sentences 3 and 5) Ask: *What makes those sentences more formal?* (e.g., word choice; sentence length) Repeat the process for the newspaper article.

- **Activity B:** Have students choose which model they would like to rewrite. Say: *Remember to keep all your sentences in the right voice for your form of writing.* Students can either rewrite the circled sentences, or insert the circled sentences from the other form of writing. Circulate to make sure that students write in a consistent voice. Then have volunteers share their revisions.

DAY 4

Read the rule aloud. Then guide students through the activity.

- Brainstorm with students interesting things they've done or seen. (e.g., sports events, trips, accomplishments, performances) Then have students pair up to interview each other.

- If necessary, model the activity by having a student interview you. Then circulate to monitor pairs.

- **Convention:** For question 5, ask: *In order to write your partner's exact words, what punctuation should you use?* (quotation marks)

DAY 5 *Writing Prompt*

- *Using the interview from Day 4, write a newspaper article about something interesting that your partner has done or seen.*

- *Be sure to use quotation marks around the exact words your partner said.*

 **Voice**   You can use formal or informal language when you write.

A. Read the e-mail message and the picture caption. They have similar purposes, but one uses *informal language* and the other uses *formal language*. Write the style of language and the audience for each one.

E-mail

Hi, Uncle Ravi!
   Here's a pic of me last Fri. at the school art show. I made this mask out of paper, paste, and paint. Wish you could come to L.A. to see it!
Hugs, Chitra

Picture Caption

   The wooden dancer's mask in this picture was created in the nineteenth century. It was made by an unknown Native American artist of the Northwest Coast.

Purpose: to tell about a mask

Style:

_____

Audience:

_____

Purpose: to tell about a mask

Style:

_____

Audience:

_____

B. Circle the quotation marks and underline the speaker's words.

   Our museum guide said, "This mask is called a raven mask. It was used by the Nakwoktak tribe."

Voice   Use a formal voice when you write a report.

A. Read Lila's school report about her trip to a museum.

> My favorite work at the museum is an ancient
> statue of Athena, the Greek goddess of war and
> wisdom. The statue shows only her head and
> shoulders. Her eyes are blank, and she has short hair.
> She is wearing loose robes and a necklace of snakes.

_____

_____

_____

_____

B. Read the sentences below. Which ones use the same language as Lila's
report? Use them to write another paragraph above for the report.

The snakes are freaky looking.

Athena is wearing a war helmet, but she does not look angry.

Maybe she is thinking about how serious war is.

You can't see her eyes, and that's totally weird.

Without eyes, you have to guess what she feels.

What is up with that goofy helmet?

C. Write what you think Lila would tell a friend about the statue.
Be sure to put quotation marks around her words.

  Lila would say, _____

_____

 **Voice**   Use the right voice throughout your writing.

A. Read the postcard and newspaper article. Circle the sentences that do not stick to the right voice.

Postcard (informal voice)

Hi Jake,

   My class went to see this play called "The Sound of Music." It was kind of weird that the characters were always singing and dancing. The musical, based on a true story, follows the courageous Von Trapp family through difficult times. A girl in my class was in it. This made the show quite special for the students!

                                                                    Brian

News Article (formal voice)

   On March 2, 2009, Ms. Murray's third-grade class attended "The Sound of Music" at Forest Theater. It's a musical about a big family trying to escape some bad guys. The cast included one of the students' classmates. That was pretty cool.

B. Rewrite the postcard or the newspaper article so that all of the sentences are in the right voice.

_____

_____

_____

_____

 **Voice** Use formal or informal language in your writing.

Interview a partner about something interesting he or she has done or seen.

1. What did you do or see?

   _____

   _____

   _____

2. When did this happen?

   _____

3. Where did it happen?

   _____

4. Whom did you go with or see?

   _____

   _____

5. Why was this so interesting or special? Write your partner's exact words.

   _____

   _____

   _____

DAY 1

Read the rule aloud. Then say: *Have you ever heard music that made you feel excited? Happy? Sad? Music can create a mood, or feeling, and so can writing. Writers create moods with words instead of sound.* Review the definition of verbs and adjectives, if necessary. Then guide students through the activities.

- **Activity A:** Explain that the rhymes on this page are called couplets, which are two-line poems that rhyme. Read the words in the box. Then read the first poem aloud. Ask: *Which word describes the mood of this poem?* (thrilling) *Why?* (poem is about an exciting scene) Have students complete the rest of the activity independently.

- **Activity B:** Have volunteers read aloud the words they wrote in Activity A to identify the mood of each couplet. Then reread the first poem and ask: *Which verbs or adjectives make the poem seem "thrilling"?* (**colorful, thrill, parading**) Repeat the process for each poem.

- **Activity C (Convention):** Say: *The first word in every line of a poem should begin with a capital letter, even if it's not a complete sentence.* Then have students complete the activity.

DAY 2

Read the rule aloud. Say: *It's important to use the mood that best fits your topic. For example, if you're writing about an exciting game you saw, make sure your writing creates excitement.* Then guide students through the activities.

- **Activity A:** Say: *A cinquain is a poem that uses adjectives and verbs to describe a topic.* Explain that **Diwali** means "rows of lighted lamps." It is a five-day festival that celebrates events in the history of India. People light lamps, visit family, and eat lots of food and sweets. Read the poem. Ask: *What mood does this poem create?* (e.g., warm) *Which words helped create that mood?* (e.g., **glowing, peaceful**) Have students underline the words.

- **Activity B:** Have students arrange the words of their choice in the poem. Say: *Choose only words that will create a joyful mood.* Remind students to capitalize the first word in each line of the poem. Ask volunteers to share their completed poems.

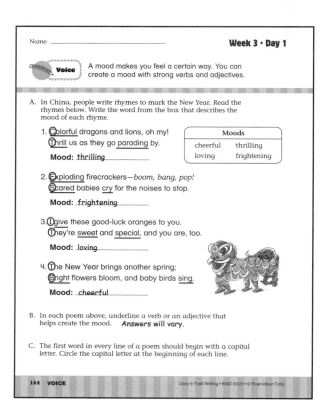

Name: _____   Week 3 · Day 1

Voice A mood makes you feel a certain way. You can create a mood with strong verbs and adjectives.

A. In China, people write rhymes to mark the New Year. Read the rhymes below. Write the word from the box that describes the mood of each rhyme.

1. Colorful dragons and lions, oh my!
   Thrill us as they go parading by.

   Mood: thrilling _____

Moods	
cheerful	thrilling
loving	frightening

2. Exploding firecrackers—*boom, bang, pop!*
   Scared babies cry for the noises to stop.

   Mood: frightening _____

3. I give these good-luck oranges to you.
   They're sweet and special, and you are, too.

   Mood: loving _____

4. The New Year brings another spring;
   Bright flowers bloom, and baby birds sing.

   Mood: cheerful _____

B. In each poem above, underline a verb or an adjective that helps create the mood.   **Answers will vary.**

C. The first word in every line of a poem should begin with a capital letter. Circle the capital letter at the beginning of each line.

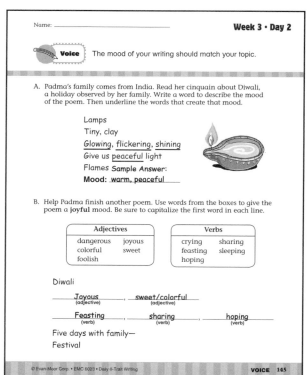

Name: _____   Week 3 · Day 2

Voice The mood of your writing should match your topic.

A. Padma's family comes from India. Read her cinquain about Diwali, a holiday observed by her family. Write a word to describe the mood of the poem. Then underline the words that create that mood.

Lamps
Tiny, clay
Glowing, flickering, shining
Give us peaceful light
Flames **Sample Answer:**
Mood: warm, peaceful _____

B. Help Padma finish another poem. Use words from the boxes to give the poem a **joyful** mood. Be sure to capitalize the first word in each line.

Adjectives			Verbs	
dangerous	joyous		crying	sharing
colorful	sweet		feasting	sleeping
foolish			hoping	

Diwali

___Joyous___ , ___sweet/colorful___
 (adjective)   (adjective)

___Feasting___ , ___sharing___ , ___hoping___
 (verb)   (verb)   (verb)

Five days with family—
Festival

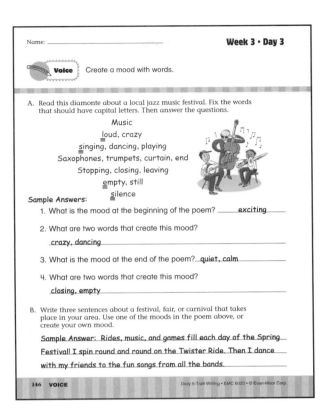

Name: _____   **Week 3 · Day 3**

Voice   Create a mood with words.

A. Read this diamonte about a local jazz music festival. Fix the words that should have capital letters. Then answer the questions.

Music
loud, crazy
singing, dancing, playing
Saxophones, trumpets, curtain, end
Stopping, closing, leaving
empty, still
silence

Sample Answers:

1. What is the mood at the beginning of the poem? _____ exciting

2. What are two words that create this mood?
   crazy, dancing

3. What is the mood at the end of the poem? quiet, calm

4. What are two words that create this mood?
   closing, empty

B. Write three sentences about a festival, fair, or carnival that takes place in your area. Use one of the moods in the poem above, or create your own mood.

Sample Answer: Rides, music, and games fill each day of the Spring Festival! I spin round and round on the Twister Ride. Then I dance with my friends to the fun songs from all the bands.

146   VOICE   Daily 6-Trait Writing • EMC 6023 • © Evan-Moor Corp.

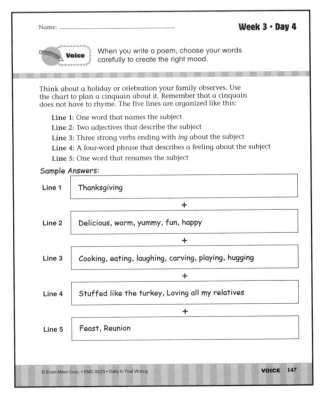

Name: _____   **Week 3 · Day 4**

Voice   When you write a poem, choose your words carefully to create the right mood.

Think about a holiday or celebration your family observes. Use the chart to plan a cinquain about it. Remember that a cinquain does not have to rhyme. The five lines are organized like this:

Line 1: One word that names the subject
Line 2: Two adjectives that describe the subject
Line 3: Three strong verbs ending with *ing* about the subject
Line 4: A four-word phrase that describes a feeling about the subject
Line 5: One word that renames the subject

Sample Answers:

Line 1	Thanksgiving

+

Line 2	Delicious, warm, yummy, fun, happy

+

Line 3	Cooking, eating, laughing, carving, playing, hugging

+

Line 4	Stuffed like the turkey, Loving all my relatives

+

Line 5	Feast, Reunion

© Evan-Moor Corp. • EMC 6023 • Daily 6-Trait Writing   **VOICE** 147

DAY 3

Read the rule aloud. Then guide students through the activities.

- **Activity A (Convention):** Say: *A diamonte is a poem that shows a change slowly occurring from the first line to the last line. It is written in the shape of a diamond.* Read the poem together. Have students mark the words that should be capitalized.

  Ask: *What change does the poem describe?* (the action at a music festival, going from full-swing to the end) Have students complete the activity and share their responses.

- **Activity B:** Brainstorm with students various local festivals, fairs, or celebrations and what happens at them. Have each student choose his or her favorite to write about. Then have volunteers read their completed sentences aloud.

DAY 4

Read the rule aloud. Then guide students through the activity.

- Read the directions aloud and refer to the model on Day 2 to review the structure of a cinquain.

- Have students name holidays or celebrations they observe. Then guide students to complete the chart with multiple answers for each line. To prompt them, ask: *What are some adjectives that can describe your holiday? What do you do on that day? Can you turn those words into **ing** action words? How do you feel about the holiday? What is another word that names your subject?*

- Have students look at the words they wrote in their chart. Ask: *Based on your words, what kind of mood will your poem probably have? Do you have a lot of exciting words? Joyful words? Peaceful words? Silly words? What kind of mood do you want to create?*

DAY 5 *Writing Prompt*

- *Write a cinquain about a celebration or holiday you observe. Use the chart you completed on Day 4 to help you.*

- *Be sure to capitalize the first word in every line of your poem.*

 **Voice** A mood makes you feel a certain way. You can create a mood with strong verbs and adjectives.

A. In China, people write rhymes to mark the New Year. Read the rhymes below. Write the word from the box that describes the mood of each rhyme.

1. Colorful dragons and lions, oh my!
   Thrill us as they go parading by.

   Mood: _____

Moods	
cheerful	thrilling
loving	frightening

2. Exploding firecrackers—*boom, bang, pop!*
   Scared babies cry for the noises to stop.

   Mood: _____

3. I give these good-luck oranges to you.
   They're sweet and special, and you are, too.

   Mood: _____

4. The New Year brings another spring;
   Bright flowers bloom, and baby birds sing.

   Mood: _____

B. In each poem above, underline a verb or an adjective that helps create the mood.

C. The first word in every line of a poem should begin with a capital letter. Circle the capital letter at the beginning of each line.

 **Voice** The mood of your writing should match your topic.

A. Padma's family comes from India. Read her cinquain about Diwali, a holiday observed by her family. Write a word to describe the mood of the poem. Then underline the words that create that mood.

Lamps
Tiny, clay
Glowing, flickering, shining
Give us peaceful light
Flames
Mood: _____

B. Help Padma finish another poem. Use words from the boxes to give the poem a **joyful** mood. Be sure to capitalize the first word in each line.

Adjectives	
dangerous	joyous
colorful	sweet
foolish	

Verbs	
crying	sharing
feasting	sleeping
hoping	

Diwali

_____ , _____
   (adjective)   (adjective)

_____ , _____ , _____
   (verb)   (verb)   (verb)

Five days with family—
Festival

 **Voice** Create a mood with words.

A. Read this diamonte about a local jazz music festival. Fix the words that should have capital letters. Then answer the questions.

Music

loud, crazy

singing, dancing, playing

Saxophones, trumpets, curtain, end

Stopping, closing, leaving

empty, still

silence

1. What is the mood at the beginning of the poem? _____

2. What are two words that create this mood?

   _____

3. What is the mood at the end of the poem?_____

4. What are two words that create this mood?

   _____

B. Write three sentences about a festival, fair, or carnival that takes place in your area. Use one of the moods in the poem above, or create your own mood.

   _____

   _____

   _____

 **Voice**

When you write a poem, choose your words carefully to create the right mood.

Think about a holiday or celebration your family observes. Use the chart to plan a cinquain about it. Remember that a cinquain does not have to rhyme. The five lines are organized like this:

Line 1: One word that names the subject

Line 2: Two adjectives that describe the subject

Line 3: Three strong verbs ending with *ing* about the subject

Line 4: A four-word phrase that describes a feeling about the subject

Line 5: One word that renames the subject

Line 1

+

Line 2

+

Line 3

+

Line 4

+

Line 5

DAY 1

Read the rule aloud. Then say: *In a story, different characters can have different points of view. Writers must choose a point of view from which to write. Do you think all of the characters in "Goldilocks and the Three Bears" would tell their story in the same way?* (no) Guide students through the activities.

- **Activity A:** Review the characters in the story "Goldilocks and the Three Bears." Then say: *Each character has his or her own particular way of seeing the events in the story.* Read statement 1 aloud. Ask: *Whose point of view is this?* (Mama Bear) *Why do you think that?* (She mentions Papa and Baby and making the porridge.) Have students complete the activity. Then discuss the answers as a class.

- **Activity B (Convention):** Say: *A prefix is a word part that can be added to the beginning of a word to make a new word. The prefixes **un-** and **dis-** mean "not" or "the opposite."* Then say: *Let's add the prefix **un-** to the base word **happy**. The word **unhappy** means "not happy."* Have students find and circle the prefixes in the words. Then ask: *What are the smaller words, or base words, that the prefixes were added to?* (**locked, agreed, broken, like**) Have students find and underline those words in Activity A.

DAY 2

Read the rule aloud. Say: *When you write from a character's point of view, use that character's voice.* Then guide students through the activities.

- **Activity A:** Read the story. Ask: *Whose point of view is this?* (the emperor's) Have students choose and write the ending that is from the emperor's point of view. Then ask: *From whose point of view are the other two endings?* (merchants'; officials') Then ask: *How are their voices different from the emperor's?* (e.g., mean; scared)

- **Activity B (Convention):** Review the meaning of the prefixes **un-** and **dis-**. Then have students complete the activity.

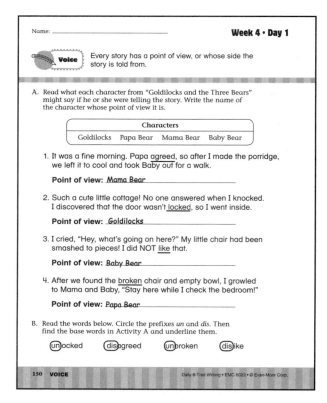

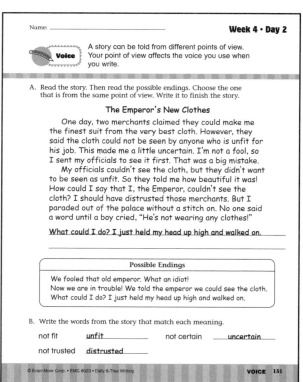

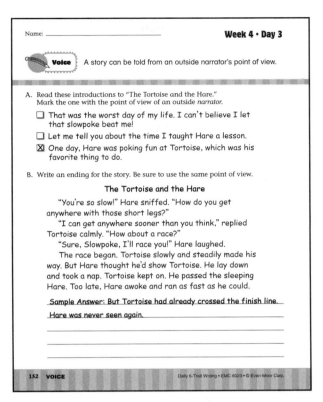

Name: _____   **Week 4 • Day 3**

Voice   A story can be told from an outside narrator's point of view.

A. Read these introductions to "The Tortoise and the Hare."
Mark the one with the point of view of an outside *narrator*.

☐ That was the worst day of my life. I can't believe I let that slowpoke beat me!

☐ Let me tell you about the time I taught Hare a lesson.

☒ One day, Hare was poking fun at Tortoise, which was his favorite thing to do.

B. Write an ending for the story. Be sure to use the same point of view.

The Tortoise and the Hare

"You're so slow!" Hare sniffed. "How do you get anywhere with those short legs?"

"I can get anywhere sooner than you think," replied Tortoise calmly. "How about a race?"

"Sure, Slowpoke, I'll race you!" Hare laughed.

The race began. Tortoise slowly and steadily made his way. But Hare thought he'd show Tortoise. He lay down and took a nap. Tortoise kept on. He passed the sleeping Hare. Too late, Hare awoke and ran as fast as he could.

Sample Answer: But Tortoise had already crossed the finish line. Hare was never seen again.

152 VOICE   Daily 6-Trait Writing • EMC 6023 • © Evan-Moor Corp.

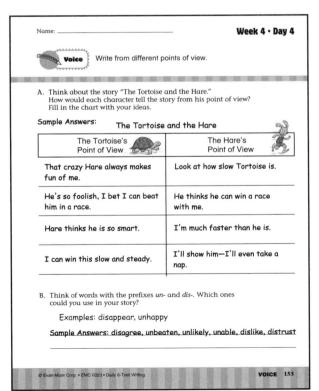

Name: _____   **Week 4 • Day 4**

Voice   Write from different points of view.

A. Think about the story "The Tortoise and the Hare." How would each character tell the story from his point of view? Fill in the chart with your ideas.

Sample Answers: The Tortoise and the Hare

The Tortoise's Point of View	The Hare's Point of View
That crazy Hare always makes fun of me.	Look at how slow Tortoise is.
He's so foolish, I bet I can beat him in a race.	He thinks he can win a race with me.
Hare thinks he is so smart.	I'm much faster than he is.
I can win this slow and steady.	I'll show him—I'll even take a nap.

B. Think of words with the prefixes *un-* and *dis-*. Which ones could you use in your story?

Examples: disappear, unhappy

Sample Answers: disagree, unbeaten, unlikely, unable, dislike, distrust

© Evan-Moor Corp. • EMC 6023 • Daily 6-Trait Writing   **VOICE 153**

DAY 3

Read the rule aloud. Say: *Some writers use the point of view of someone outside the story, called a* **narrator.** *The narrator may know more about what is happening than the characters do.* Guide students through the activities.

- **Activity A:** Briefly review the story "The Tortoise and the Hare." Then read the introductions aloud. Ask: *Which one sounds like it is from the point of view of a narrator, or someone outside the story?* ("One day...," because it does not use **I** and does not show personal emotion)

- **Activity B:** Read the story aloud. Ask: *Whose point of view is this?* (narrator) *How do you know?* (e.g., doesn't use the pronoun **I** outside of dialogue; knows what every character is doing) Then have students write their own endings. Remind them to keep the same point of view and voice as that of the story.

DAY 4

Read the rule aloud. Then guide students through the activities.

- **Activity A:** Say: *Yesterday, we read "The Tortoise and the Hare" from the point of view of an outside narrator. But what if Tortoise or Hare told the story? They had very different ways of looking at things. Use your imagination to fill in the chart with statements from each animal's point of view at different times in the story. For example, at the beginning of the story, Hare makes fun of Tortoise. Hare might say, "Look at how slow Tortoise is." But at the same time, Tortoise might be thinking, "That crazy Hare always makes fun of me."*

- **Activity B (Convention):** Brainstorm words with the prefixes **un-** and **dis-**. If necessary, have students look back at the activities on Days 1 and 2 to find words with **un-** and **dis-**.

DAY 5 *Writing Prompt*

- *Use your chart from Day 4 to rewrite the story "The Tortoise and the Hare." Tell it from the point of view of one of the characters.*

- *Try to use a word with the prefix* **un-** *or* **dis-**.

 **Voice**   Every story has a point of view, or whose side the story is told from.

A. Read what each character from "Goldilocks and the Three Bears" might say if he or she were telling the story. Write the name of the character whose point of view it is.

> **Characters**
>
> Goldilocks   Papa Bear   Mama Bear   Baby Bear

1. It was a fine morning. Papa agreed, so after I made the porridge, we left it to cool and took Baby out for a walk.

   Point of view: _____

2. Such a cute little cottage! No one answered when I knocked. I discovered that the door wasn't locked, so I went inside.

   Point of view: _____

3. I cried, "Hey, what's going on here?" My little chair had been smashed to pieces! I did NOT like that.

   Point of view: _____

4. After we found the broken chair and empty bowl, I growled to Mama and Baby, "Stay here while I check the bedroom!"

   Point of view: _____

B. Read the words below. Circle the prefixes *un* and *dis*. Then find the base words in Activity A and underline them.

   unlocked   disagreed   unbroken   dislike

 **Voice**   A story can be told from different points of view. Your point of view affects the voice you use when you write.

A. Read the story. Then read the possible endings. Choose the one that is from the same point of view. Write it to finish the story.

The Emperor's New Clothes

One day, two merchants claimed they could make me the finest suit from the very best cloth. However, they said the cloth could not be seen by anyone who is unfit for his job. This made me a little uncertain. I'm not a fool, so I sent my officials to see it first. That was a big mistake.

My officials couldn't see the cloth, but they didn't want to be seen as unfit. So they told me how beautiful it was! How could I say that I, the Emperor, couldn't see the cloth? I should have distrusted those merchants. But I paraded out of the palace without a stitch on. No one said a word until a boy cried, "He's not wearing any clothes!"

_____

_____

Possible Endings
We fooled that old emperor. What an idiot!
Now we are in trouble! We told the emperor we could see the cloth.
What could I do? I just held my head up high and walked on.

B. Write the words from the story that match each meaning.

not fit   _____   not certain   _____

not trusted   _____

 **Voice** A story can be told from an outside narrator's point of view.

A. Read these introductions to "The Tortoise and the Hare."
   Mark the one with the point of view of an outside *narrator*.

☐ That was the worst day of my life. I can't believe I let that slowpoke beat me!

☐ Let me tell you about the time I taught Hare a lesson.

☐ One day, Hare was poking fun at Tortoise, which was his favorite thing to do.

B. Write an ending for the story. Be sure to use the same point of view.

The Tortoise and the Hare

"You're so slow!" Hare sniffed. "How do you get anywhere with those short legs?"

"I can get anywhere sooner than you think," replied Tortoise calmly. "How about a race?"

"Sure, Slowpoke, I'll race you!" Hare laughed.

The race began. Tortoise slowly and steadily made his way. But Hare thought he'd show Tortoise. He lay down and took a nap. Tortoise kept on. He passed the sleeping Hare. Too late, Hare awoke and ran as fast as he could.

_____

_____

_____

_____

_____

 **Voice**   Write from different points of view.

A. Think about the story "The Tortoise and the Hare."
   How would each character tell the story from his point of view?
   Fill in the chart with your ideas.

The Tortoise and the Hare

The Tortoise's Point of View	The Hare's Point of View

B. Think of words with the prefixes *un-* and *dis-*. Which ones
   could you use in your story?

   Examples: disappear, unhappy

   _____

   _____

DAY 1

Read the rule aloud. Say: *Remember that your voice is what comes through in your writing. It shows your reader who you are and how you feel.* Then guide students through the activity.

- Read both stories aloud. Then guide students through the questions, prompting them to provide concrete answers. For example, ask: *How did Le make you feel you were there? What did he do that Tam did not?* (used sensory details and sounds; described his actions) Finally, ask: *Which story has a stronger voice?* (Le's)

- **Convention:** Have students find this sentence in Le's story: *"Just making sure, I told him."* Point out the comma after what was actually said and have students circle it. Say: *In dialogue, the comma always comes before the quotation mark.* Then rewrite the sentence on the board this way: *I told him, "Just making sure."* and have students point out the comma.

DAY 2

Read the rule aloud. Say: *In order for your voice to shine through your writing, you should be honest and say what you really think and feel.* Then guide students through the activities.

- **Activity A (Convention):** Read the story aloud. Have students find the lines of dialogue without commas. Point them out and ask: *Where should the commas go?* (inside the quotation marks) Circulate to make sure that students write the commas in the proper places. Explain that lines of dialogue ending with exclamation points or question marks do <u>not</u> need commas.

- **Activity B:** Ask: *Can you imagine eating carrot and sweet potato pizza? What would you think if someone served it to you? What would you tell someone about it?* Then have students write their own reactions.

  Ask volunteers to share what they wrote. Point out the variety of answers. Say: *Each of your unique answers shows who you are. They show your voice.* If students' reactions do not seem realistic or honest, prompt them to write a more authentic answer. Ask: *Is that really what you would think? Would you actually say that to someone?*

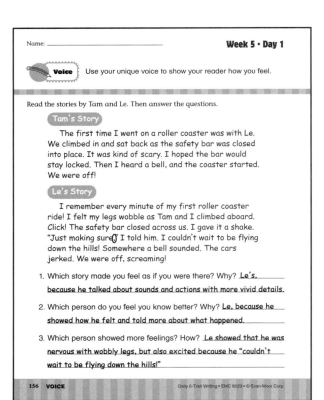

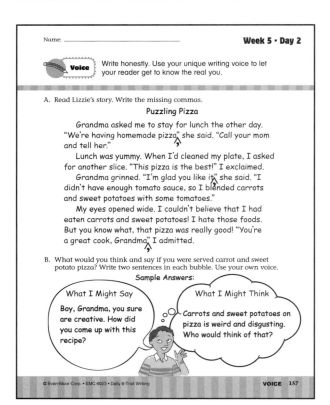

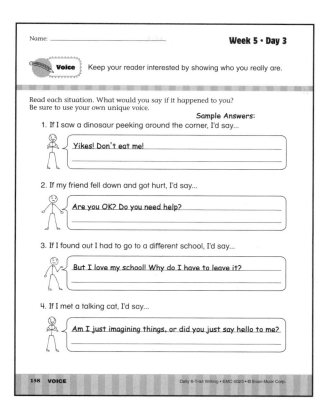

Name: _____

Week 5 • Day 3

Voice Keep your reader interested by showing who you really are.

Read each situation. What would you say if it happened to you?
Be sure to use your own unique voice.

Sample Answers:

1. If I saw a dinosaur peeking around the corner, I'd say...

Yikes! Don't eat me!

2. If my friend fell down and got hurt, I'd say...

Are you OK? Do you need help?

3. If I found out I had to go to a different school, I'd say...

But I love my school! Why do I have to leave it?

4. If I met a talking cat, I'd say...

Am I just imagining things, or did you just say hello to me?

158 VOICE   Daily 6-Trait Writing • EMC 6023 • © Evan-Moor Corp.

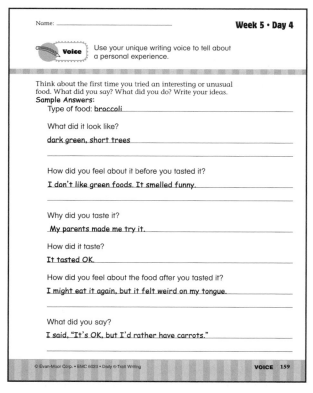

Name: _____

Week 5 • Day 4

Voice Use your unique writing voice to tell about a personal experience.

Think about the first time you tried an interesting or unusual food. What did you say? What did you do? Write your ideas.

Sample Answers:

Type of food: broccoli

What did it look like?

dark green, short trees

How did you feel about it before you tasted it?

I don't like green foods. It smelled funny.

Why did you taste it?

My parents made me try it.

How did it taste?

It tasted OK.

How did you feel about the food after you tasted it?

I might eat it again, but it felt weird on my tongue.

What did you say?

I said, "It's OK, but I'd rather have carrots."

© Evan-Moor Corp. • EMC 6023 • Daily 6-Trait Writing   VOICE 159

DAY 3

Read the rule aloud. Say: *When you show who you really are and say what you really think, your reader will be more interested in your writing.* Then guide students through the activity.

- Write these sentences on the board and ask: *Which one has a stronger voice? Which sounds more interesting? 1) I don't like asparagus. 2) I sure hope we're not having asparagus for dinner.* (sentence 2) Say: *Imagining what you would really say in a situation can help your voice shine through when you write.*

- Read the first situation. Say: *If I saw a dinosaur on the street, I would be pretty terrified. I'd probably say, "Whoa, where did you come from? Please don't eat me!"* Have students complete the activity independently and read aloud their responses.

DAY 4

Read the rule aloud. Then guide students through the activity.

- Invite students to share their experiences trying new or unusual foods. For example, ask: *Did your parents ever make you eat a vegetable you didn't like? Have you ever tried a new dish from a different country?* Then have them think deeper about the experience by completing the questionnaire. Provide assistance and further prompts, if necessary.

- **Convention:** For the last question, encourage students to write their answer in dialogue form. Check to make sure they put the comma in the proper place.

DAY 5 *Writing Prompt*

- *Use the questionnaire you completed on Day 4 to write about a time you tried a food for the first time. Let your own voice come out in your writing.*

- *Be sure to place commas before quotation marks in dialogue.*

 **Voice** Use your unique voice to show your reader how you feel.

Read the stories by Tam and Le. Then answer the questions.

Tam's Story

The first time I went on a roller coaster was with Le. We climbed in and sat back as the safety bar was closed into place. It was kind of scary. I hoped the bar would stay locked. Then I heard a bell, and the coaster started. We were off!

Le's Story

I remember every minute of my first roller coaster ride! I felt my legs wobble as Tam and I climbed aboard. Click! The safety bar closed across us. I gave it a shake. "Just making sure," I told him. I couldn't wait to be flying down the hills! Somewhere a bell sounded. The cars jerked. We were off, screaming!

1. Which story made you feel as if you were there? Why? _____

_____

2. Which person do you feel you know better? Why? _____

_____

3. Which person showed more feelings? How? _____

_____

_____

Voice Write honestly. Use your unique writing voice to let your reader get to know the real you.

A. Read Lizzie's story. Write the missing commas.

Puzzling Pizza

Grandma asked me to stay for lunch the other day. "We're having homemade pizza" she said. "Call your mom and tell her."

Lunch was yummy. When I'd cleaned my plate, I asked for another slice. "This pizza is the best!" I exclaimed.

Grandma grinned. "I'm glad you like it" she said. "I didn't have enough tomato sauce, so I blended carrots and sweet potatoes with some tomatoes."

My eyes opened wide. I couldn't believe that I had eaten carrots and sweet potatoes! I hate those foods. But you know what, that pizza was really good! "You're a great cook, Grandma" I admitted.

B. What would you think and say if you were served carrot and sweet potato pizza? Write two sentences in each bubble. Use your own voice.

What I Might Say

What I Might Think

 **Voice** · Keep your reader interested by showing who you really are.

Read each situation. What would you say if it happened to you?
Be sure to use your own unique voice.

1. If I saw a dinosaur peeking around the corner, I'd say...

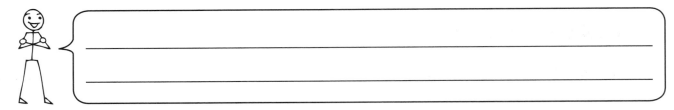

2. If my friend fell down and got hurt, I'd say...

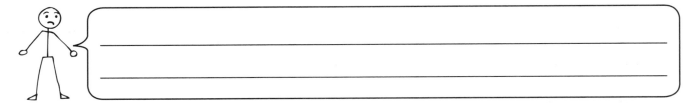

3. If I found out I had to go to a different school, I'd say...

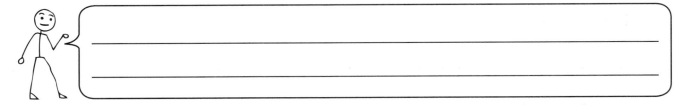

4. If I met a talking cat, I'd say...

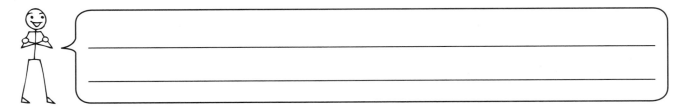

Voice Use your unique writing voice to tell about a personal experience.

Think about the first time you tried an interesting or unusual food. What did you say? What did you do? Write your ideas.

Type of food: _____

What did it look like?

_____

_____

How did you feel about it before you tasted it?

_____

_____

Why did you taste it?

_____

How did it taste?

_____

How did you feel about the food after you tasted it?

_____

_____

What did you say?

_____

_____

Proofreading Marks

Mark	Meaning	Example
℘	Take this out (delete).	I love ℘ to read.
⊙	Add a period.	It was late⊙
≡	Make this a capital letter.	First prize went to maria.
/	Make this a lowercase letter.	We saw a Black Cat.
___	Fix the spelling.	This is our ~~hause~~. (house)
⋏	Add a comma.	Goodnight⋏Mom.
⌄	Add an apostrophe.	That⌄s Lil⌄s bike.
! ? ⋀ ⋀	Add an exclamation point or a question mark.	Help⋀Can you help me⋀
⋀	Add a word or a letter.	The⋀pen is mine. (red)
# ⋀	Add a space between words.	I like⋀pizza.
___	Underline the words.	We read Old Yeller.
⌄ ⌄	Add quotation marks.	⌄Come in,⌄he said.